Simon Sechter

The Correct Order of Fundamental Harmonies

a treatise on fundamental basses and their inversions and substitutes

Simon Sechter

The Correct Order of Fundamental Harmonies
a treatise on fundamental basses and their inversions and substitutes

ISBN/EAN: 9783743359864

Manufactured in Europe, USA, Canada, Australia, Japa

Cover: Foto ©Thomas Meinert / pixelio.de

Manufactured and distributed by brebook publishing software (www.brebook.com)

Simon Sechter

The Correct Order of Fundamental Harmonies

THE

CORRECT ORDER

OF

FUNDAMENTAL HARMONIES:

A TREATISE

ON

Fundamental Basses, and their Inversions and Substitutes.

FROM THE GERMAN OF

S. SECHTER,

LATE IMPERIAL COURT-ORGANIST, AND PROFESSOR OF HARMONY IN THE CONSERVATORY OF MUSIC
AT VIENNA.

THE WHOLE COMPILED AND ADAPTED FOR POPULAR USE

By C. C. MÜLLER.

NEW YORK:
Published by WM. A. POND & CO., 547 Broadway.
1871.

PREFACE.

———

THE extensive patronage which is extended to the Musical Art by the American Public, and which has encouraged so many to apply themselves to the noble study of Musical Composition, may be pleaded as an apology for the appearance of a new treatise on Harmony.

The present work, which has been compiled, and adapted for popular use, from the celebrated treatise by S. SECHTER, entitled : *Die richtige Folge der Grundharmonien*, etc., aims solely to elucidate the *formation of harmonic progressions*, and to present the *means of modulation;* leaving untouched, for the present, the subjects of Melody and Counterpoint.

The treatise begins with the discussion of the harmonic progressions in the *diatonic major scale.* Next is shown the peculiar nature of the *diatonic minor scale*, and the means of *diatonic modulation* are pointed out. Hereupon follow, the elucidation of the *chromatic progressions*, both in the major and minor scales ; and lastly, that of the *enharmonic changes.*

The circumstance that SECHTER's work was intended chiefly for teachers and advanced students, necessitated, in this translation, certain deviations from the original, especially in Part I, such as, the insertion of the sections elucidating the elementary principles of harmony, involving, again, a different disposition of the subject matter, with a view to the most gradual development, and to the presentation in the clearest manner possible, of SECHTER's system. Moreover, at the ends of Parts I and II, the student will find, among other directions, a table suggestive of exercises for practice, applicable also to Parts IV and V ; an addition which, it is hoped, will compensate for the omission of many repetitions, redundant examples, etc., which was deemed advisable in a work intended for popular use.

The compiler would here acknowledge with the deepest gratitude the valuable assistance which Mr. J. H. CORNELL has rendered him in the translation of SECHTER's work. It will be in great part owing to his interest in the Treatise, his knowledge of the subject, and his indefatigable and conscientious pains-taking, if this work, the fruit of much love and many sacrifices, should meet with the success which the name of SECHTER ought to assure to it.

The compiler's thanks are also due to Mr. J. W. TAYLOR, the stereotyper, for his promptness and many courtesies (his typography, by the bye, speaks for itself)—also to Mr. WM. A. POND, the publisher, for the liberality to which the public are indebted for the getting up of the work.

C. C. MÜLLER.

NEW YORK, *January 1, 1871*

CONTENTS.

PART I.

GENERAL REMARKS, AND PROGRESSIONS IN THE DIATONIC MAJOR SCALE.

———

PART II.

HARMONIC PROGRESSIONS IN THE DIATONIC MINOR SCALE.

PART III.

DIATONIC MODULATION.

PART IV.

CHROMATIC PROGRESSIONS IN THE SCALE OF C MAJOR.

PART V.

CHROMATIC PROGRESSIONS IN THE SCALE OF A MINOR.

PART VI.

OF ENHARMONIC CHANGES.

PART I.

GENERAL REMARKS,

AND

PROGRESSIONS IN THE DIATONIC MAJOR SCALE.

SECTION I.

A TREATISE on harmony properly commences with the definition of INTERVALS.

The term *interval* expresses that relation in which one tone stands to another with regard to the *difference of pitch*.

NOTE.—We use the word *tone* in its strict sense, as signifying a *sound*, not an interval. Instead of the word *tone*, as generally, but incorrectly used, we adopt the expression *whole step*, or simply *step*.

The interval is directly determined according to the respective positions of the two tones upon the staff. Thus, we have two tones, each written upon a different degree of the staff, the *lower* of which is generally reckoned as standing, for the time being (*i. e.* in respect to the *higher tone*), upon the *first* degree. The relation of the higher to the lower tone—in other words, the interval—is determined by the number of degrees involved in their difference of pitch. We have, for instance, the two tones, D and the G above it. Counting D as *one*, we pass through the degrees E (two) and F (three), till we arrive at G, four. G is therefore a *fourth* in respect to D below it.

The smallest interval is that which forms a *half-step*.

The *half-step* is either *chromatic* or *diatonic*.

The *chromatic half-step* is a progression from one tone to another, both of which are written upon the same degree (*a*). The *diatonic half-step* is a progression from one tone to another, one of which is written on the degree immediately above the other (*b*), *e. g.:*

(a) Chromatic Half-steps.   **(b) Diatonic Half-steps.**

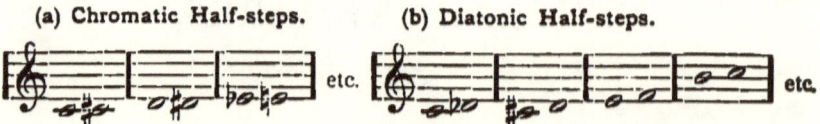

A *step* is a progression from one tone to another, involving an inaudible chromatic half-step, *e. g.:*

SECTION II.

An ascending or descending intermingled succession of five steps and two diatonic half-steps constitutes a *scale*, *e. g.:*

The most simple scale, characterized by the major third and major sixth, is that which ascends from the 1st to the 2d degree, one step; from the 2d to the 3d degree, one step; from the 3d to the 4th, one diatonic half-step; from the 4th to the 5th, one step; from the 5th to the 6th, one step; from the 6th to the 7th, one step; and from the 7th to the 8th, one diatonic half-step, and descends again in the same order, *e. g.:*

This scale, in which the two diatonic half-steps occur between the 3d and 4th, and between the 7th and 8th degrees, respectively, is called the *major scale*, to the discussion of which this first part is exclusively devoted.

That major scale which begins with C, as being the simplest, requiring no flats or sharps in its construction, will be taken as the *model scale*, in which all the examples in this work will be given.

Each degree has its own name: the 1st is called *Tonic ;* the 2d, *Second ;* the 3d, *Mediant ;* the 4th, *Sub-dominant ;* the 5th, *Dominant ;* the 6th, *Sub-mediant ;* and the 7th, *Leading tone.* The most important of these are : the *tonic,* the *dominant,* and the *sub-dominant.*

Each degree may be changed into a tonic of a major scale, provided the order of successive degrees, as explained above, is adhered to. This change is made by means of the accidentals : *sharps* (♯), and *flats* (♭), *e. g. :*

etc.   etc.

SECTION III.

Tones which form an essential part of the scale are called *Diatonic tones, e. g. :*

Tones which are foreign to the *Diatonic scale,* are named *Chromatic tones, e. g. :*

Tones standing on different degrees, yet producing the same sound, are known as *Enharmonic* tones, *e. g. :*

etc.

Part I will treat of the *Diatonic major scale* only.

SECTION IV.

The major scale contains the following intervals :

1st.—The *perfect prime* (*unison*), the two tones of which must invariably stand on the same degree, *e. g.*:

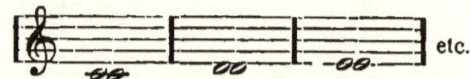

NOTE.—It is evident that in the case of the perfect prime there is, strictly speaking, no interval.

2d.—*Seconds* are intervals from one degree to the next one above. They are (*a*) *minor*, if the distance between the two tones forming the second is that of a diatonic half-step, or (*b*) *major*, if it is that of a step, *e. g.*:

   (a) Minor Seconds.   (b) Major Seconds.

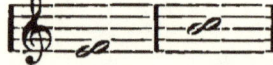 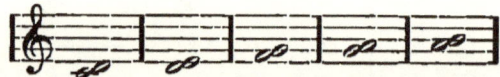

3d.—*Thirds* are intervals from one degree to the second above. They are : (*a*) *minor*, if the distance between the two tones forming a third is that of a step and a diatonic half-step, or (*b*) *major*, if it is that of two steps, *e. g.*:

   (a) Minor Thirds.   (b) Major Thirds.

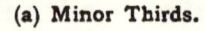 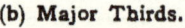

4th.—*Fourths* are intervals from one degree to the third above. They are: (*a*) *perfect*, if the distance between the two tones is that of two steps and a diatonic half-step, or (*b*) *augmented*, if it is that of three steps. This latter is called *Tritonus*, and in the major scale occurs only between the 4th and 7th degrees, *e. g.*:

   (a) Perfect Fourths.   (b) Augmented Fourth.

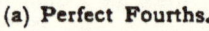 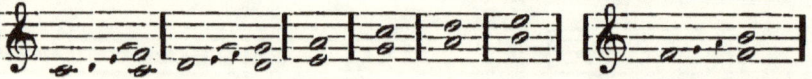

5th.—*Fifths* are intervals from one degree to the fourth above, and are : (*a*) *diminished*, if the distance between the two tones is that of two steps and two diatonic half-steps (the diatonic major scale containing only one, *i. e.*

between the 7th and 4th, *i. e.* 11th, degrees), or (*b*) *perfect*, if it is that of three steps and one diatonic half-step, *e. g.*:

(a) **Diminished Fifth.**   (b) **Perfect Fifths.**

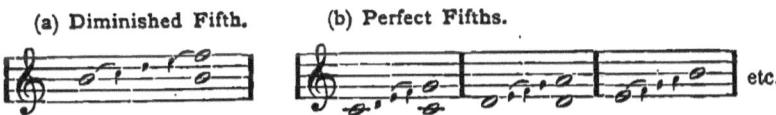

etc.

6th.—*Sixths* are intervals from one degree to the fifth above, and are : (*a*) *minor*, if the distance between the two tones is that of three steps and two diatonic half-steps, or (*b*) *major*, if it is that of four steps and one diatonic half-step, *e. g.*:

(a) **Minor Sixths.**   (b) **Major Sixths.**

7th.—*Sevenths* are intervals from one degree to the sixth above, and are (*a*) *minor*, if the distance between the two tones is that of four steps and two diatonic half-steps, or (*b*) *major*, if it is that of five steps and one diatonic half-step, *e. g.*:

(a) **Minor Sevenths.**   (b) **Major Sevenths.**

8th.—*Octaves* are intervals from one degree to the seventh above. In the diatonic major scale they only occur *perfect*, the distance between the two tones being that of five steps and two diatonic half-steps, *e.g.*:

Perfect Octaves.

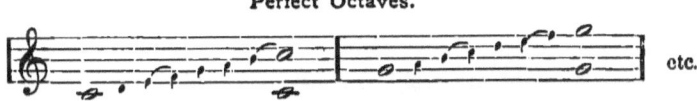

etc.

9th.—*Ninths* are intervals from one degree to the eighth above. They are : (*a*) *minor*, if the distance between the two tones is that of five steps and three diatonic half-steps ; or (*b*) *major*, if it is that of six steps and two diatonic half-steps, *e. g.*:

(a) **Minor Ninths.**   (b) **Major Ninths.**

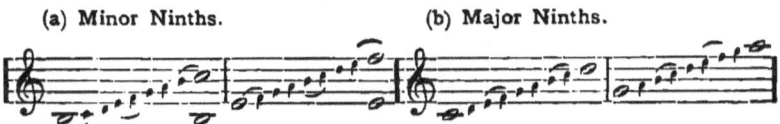

The extension of a major scale by an octave will produce every desirable proportion, *e. g. :*

The tones from the 8th degree to the 15th, bear the same names as those from the 1st, to the 8th degree; a peculiar relationship, however, will sometimes arise between the tones of an upper and those of a lower octave. This will be discussed under the head of *suspensions.*

SECTION V.

The intervals are indicated by ciphers. *E. g.,* if one voice gives the tone : and another is to sound its perfect prime, then the figuring will be : when its effect is :

If one voice has to sound a second to another voice, the figuring is and the effect is : The interval of a third is fig-ured : and so on to the fifteenth :

which is the greatest interval that occurs. This way of expressing notes by ciphers is known by the name of *Figuring,* or *Thorough-Bass notation.*

SECTION VI.

An *inversion* arises when of two tones the lower one is transposed above the upper one, *e. g. :*

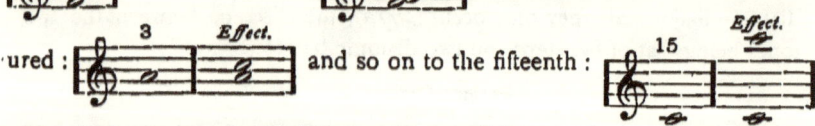

changing the upper tone to be bass, and the fundamental to be upper tone. All intervals, within the space of an octave, may be inverted in this manner :

·Expressed in ciphers :

The inversion of   1, 2, 3, 4, 5, 6, 7, 8.
       gives   8, 7, 6, 5, 4, 3, 2, 1.

Inverted perfect intervals remain *perfect;* major intervals become *minor;* minor intervals become *major;* the diminished become *augmented;* and the augmented become *diminished.*

SECTION VII.

The character of the major scale depends upon the perfect tuning of the perfect upper fifth and major upper third of the tonic, dominant and sub-dominant. *E. g.*, if C is the tonic of the major scale, the dominant (G), which occurs as its perfect upper fifth, has to be tuned perfect. The next important tone of the scale is the sub-dominant (F), which occurs as perfect under-fifth of C, and must also be tuned perfect, as must also the fifth (D) of the dominant (G). Then the major thirds, *e*, of the tonic, *b*, of the dominant, and *a*, of the sub-dominant, must be tuned perfect. But since *a* was tuned as major third of F, and D as perfect fifth of G, without regard to each other, it follows that the fifth, D-*a*, possesses not that perfect character of the other perfect fifths, the D having become too high by the ninth part of a step ; thus bringing the two tones that much nearer to each other, which *fifth* may then be designated as the *Dubious fifth.* Each of the fifths of the tonic, dominant, and sub-dominant, forms, in relation to the perfect major thirds of their fundamentals, a perfect minor third, but F having been tuned as perfect under-fifth of C, and D having been tuned as perfect upper-fifth of G, without regard to each other, they have as minor-third not that perfect proportion, because their distance is short by one ninth part of a step, *e. g.*:

Perfect Fifth.   Perfect Fifth.   Minor Third.

Major Third. Minor Third. Major Third. Minor Third. Perfect Octave. Dubious Fifth. Major Third. Perfect Fifth.

Nevertheless, it would be a great error to suppose for an instant, that the character of the fifth of the 2d degree is dubious, exclusively in the scale of C major, since every other major scale (speaking theoretically), would require to be tuned in the same manner, and since we should arrive at the same results.

Although, according to the above explanation, the Piano-forte does not exactly correspond with the perfect system of the major scale, (the tones being tuned in general with regard to each other, and in such a way as to produce all the different scales in as nearly perfect a proportion as possible, which in fact is the sole characteristic of the tempered system,) yet, the theory of the perfect system must be strictly adhered to.

SECTION VIII.

The intervals in Sec. IV are divided into two classes, viz: *Consonances* and *Dissonances.*

Consonances are intervals whose tones bear a satisfactory relation to each other. They are either *complete*, or *incomplete.*

Complete consonances are the *perfect prime*, the *perfect fifth* (that of the 2d degree excepted), the *perfect octave*, and the *perfect fourth* (that of the 6th degree excepted, because the inversion of the dubious fifth of the 2d degree results in the dubious fourth of the 6th degree).

Incomplete consonances, are the *minor* and *major third*, and the *minor* and *major sixth.*

The *Consonances* may enter free and unprepared ;* they require no resolution, and may be doubled, except the dubious fifth of the 2d degree, which must be prepared, and resolved one degree downward, and cannot be doubled.

Dissonances are intervals whose tones do not bear a satisfactory relation to each other. To this class belong the *minor* and *major second*, the *diminished fifth*, the *augmented fourth*, the *minor* and *major seventh*, and the *minor* and *major ninth.*

The dissonances must be prepared and resolved. The *preparation* takes place when a tone occurs as consonance in the first, and remains as dissonance in the second chord. The *resolution* of a dissonance is effected by the progression of the dissonant tone to the next degree below or above.

Dissonances admit of no doubling. Dissonances become the more dissonant the greater the distance between them and the fundamental. Hence, a seventh is more dissonant than a diminished fifth ; and a ninth is more dissonant than a seventh, etc.

---

* With regard to the *fourth*, see Sec. XI. 2d.

By maintaining its position, whilst other tones progress, a dissonance may become more dissonant (*a*), but it can never become a consonance (*b*).

(a)   (b) Faulty.

SECTION IX.

Two tones, progressing by degrees, form a *melodic step.** Several successive melodic steps form a *melodic passage.*   *Simultaneous* sounds, of two or more tones, are termed *chords.*   A succession of chords, formed according to theoretical rules, we call *harmony,* or a *harmonic passage.*

SECTION X.

A *primary chord* is formed when the third of one *fundamental* stands at the same time as *fundamental* to another third.

A *simultaneous sound* of three tones, arranged as above, forms a *triad* (*a*).

A *simultaneous sound* of four tones, similarly arranged, forms a *chord of the seventh* (*b*).

(a)   (b)

The above two chords are the only *primary* chords : from these all others are derived.

SECTION XI.

The 1st, 5th, and 4th degrees of the major scale are fundamental to *major triads,* each having a major third and perfect fifth :

They are the most important, and may enter free and unprepared.

The 2d, 3d and 6th degrees are fundamental to *minor triads,* each having a minor third and perfect fifth :

* The word "step," in this sense, is used in contradistinction to the *skip.*

The triads of the 3d and 6th degrees may enter free and unprepared; but the dubious fifth of the 2d degree must be prepared, and resolved one degree downward. It is prepared, if the triad of the 2d degree is preceded by that of the 6th or of the 4th degree, and resolved, if it is followed by that of the 5th degree, *e. g.*:

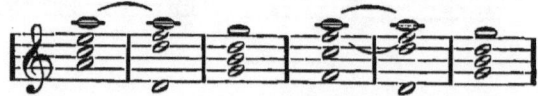

The 7th degree is fundamental to a *diminished triad*, containing a minor third and diminished fifth :  The *diminished fifth*, being a 'dissonance, *must be prepared, and resolved one degree downward.* It is prepared, if the triad of the 7th is preceded by that of the 4th degree, and resolved, if it is followed by that of the 3d degree, *e. g.*:

In forming a four-voiced chord from a triad, one of its three component tones must be doubled, or, most usually, added in the octave.

The tone of the triad best adapted for duplication is the *fundamental;* the next best is its *third;* and the last may be the *fifth*, provided it does not occur dubious or diminished.

The *most essential* tones of the triad are the *fundamental* and the *third;* the *fifth* may be omitted.

The triad needs no figuring.

From the triad we derive the following *inversions :*

1st.—If the octave of the fundamental is transposed above the third, leaving the third as *bass*, we have the *chord of the sixth*. It consists of a third and sixth of the bass, being marked 6, thereby including the third.

NOTE.—In all cases of inversions, the *fundamental* will be indicated by capital letters under the staff.

It may enter free and unprepared. The intervals best suited for duplications, are : *The sixth (original fundamental) ;* the bass, (*original third*); and lastly :' the *third* (*original fifth*).

2d.—If the *octave* and the *third* are transposed above the *fifth*, leaving the fifth as bass, we have the *chord of the fourth* and *sixth.* It consists of the *fourth* and *sixth* of the bass, and is marked ⁶₄. This chord can occur only when either the *bass* (*original fifth*) or its *fourth* is prepared, in which case the *bass* must resolve either one degree upward, or one degree downward.

It·is well to resolve the bass upward, if it is prepared from below, or downward, if from above.

This chord requires, at first, the doubling of the *fourth* (*original fundamental*), then that of the *sixth* (*original third*), and lastly that of the *bass.*

These inversions do not alter the character of the dubious fifth of the 2d, or that of the diminished fifth of the 7th degree, which must be prepared and resolved, whether they occur in the primary chord or in an inversion.

SECTION XII.

The *chord of the seventh* is formed by the simultaneous sound of three thirds, placed one above the other. Hence it consists of the *third, fifth* and *seventh* of the fundamental, and is marked 7, which includes the third and fifth. Its component tones may be doubled, as follows : at first the fundamental ; then the third, and lastly the fifth, provided the latter is not dubious or diminished. The seventh, being a dissonance, and requiring to be resolved downwards, cannot be doubled. The fifth may be omitted.

The chord of the seventh of the 5th degree is called the *dominant chord of the seventh*, and consists of a *major third, perfect fifth*, and *minor seventh.* It is the most harmonious of all chords of the seventh, and occurs oftenest, and therefore is called the *primary chord of the seventh.* It is the only one that can enter free, while all other sevenths must be prepared ; but *all sevenths* must be resolved one degree downward.

The major scale contains the following additional chords of the seventh :

The 1st and 4th degrees are fundamental to a chord of the seventh, consisting of a major triad and a major seventh (*a*).

The 2d, 3d, and 6th degrees are fundamental to a chord of the seventh, consisting of a minor triad, and a minor seventh (*b*).

The 7th degree is fundamental to a chord of the seventh, consisting of a diminished triad and a minor seventh (*c*).

Primary Chord of the 7th.   (*a*)   (*b*)   (*c*)

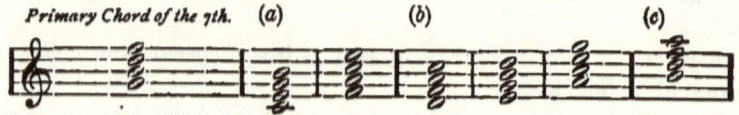

The preparation of a seventh takes place most naturally when the fundamental of the chord preceding occurs a fifth higher (or a fourth lower) than that which contains the seventh. In this manner the third of the first remains as seventh of the second fundamental.

The resolution of the seventh is effected when the chord containing a seventh is followed by another whose fundamental occurs a fifth lower (or a fourth higher) than that which contains the seventh. The seventh of the first will then resolve into the third of the second fundamental.

Primary Chord of the 7th. Resolution.   *Preparation. Chord of the 7th.   Resolution.*

From the chord of the seventh the following inversions are derived :

1st.—If the *octave* of the fundamental is transposed above its *third*, leaving the latter as bass, we have *the chord of the fifth and sixth*, consisting of a *third*, *fifth* and *sixth*. It is marked $\frac{6}{5}$, which includes the third. The *fifth* of this chord, being the original seventh of the chord of the seventh, must be prepared, and resolved one degree downward. All the other tones retain their qualities, original and fundamental. This chord may occur without its third.

Fund. D   G   C   G   C   F   B   E   A   E   A   D

2d.—If the *octave* and the *third* of the fundamental are transposed above the *fifth*, leaving the latter as bass, we have the *chord of the third and fourth*, consisting of a *third, fourth* and *sixth*, marked ⁴₃, which includes the sixth. In this chord the original seventh appears as *third*, which accordingly must be prepared and resolved. This chord must appear four-voiced, and requires the same treatment as the chord of the fourth and sixth.

3d.—If the *octave, third* and *fifth* of the fundamental are transposed above its *seventh*, leaving the latter as bass, we have the *chord of the second.* It consists of the *second, fourth and sixth*, and is marked 2, which includes the fourth and sixth. Here the original seventh appears as bass, which therefore must be prepared and resolved, *e. g. :*

The inversions of the dominant chord of the seventh may enter free and unprepared, provided no other rule is violated; but that tone which takes the place of the seventh, must always be resolved one degree downward.

SECTION XIII.

The *chord of the ninth* consists of the *third, fifth* and *ninth* of the fundamental, and is marked 9, which includes the third and fifth. The fundamental, third, and fifth, being consonances, may enter free and be doubled, provided the fifth is not dubious nor diminished. The ninth, being a dissonance, must be prepared, and resolve one degree downward, and cannot be doubled. (Sec. XL.)

The ninth can never appear close to the octave of the fundamental, nor below, but must invariably occur as the actual ninth to that voice which sounds the fundamental. The dubious and diminished fifth must always occur in a higher voice than the ninth, as otherwise progressions of parallel fifths would be the result. (Sec. XXIII.)

NOTE.—The chord of the *ninth* should never be mistaken for the chord of the *second.*

SECTION XIV.

Here it should be mentioned, that the four-voiced harmony is the most usual, although harmonies which are more or fewer-voiced are admissible. The upper voice is termed *Soprano,* the next below, *Alto,* the next below, *Tenor,* and the lowest, *Bass.* The leading of the Bass must be effected according to the strictest rules, particularly in the case of the alternate employment of primary and inverted chords. To enable us to proceed correctly, it is absolutely necessary to bear the primary chords distinctly in mind, to which end we indicate the *fundamental* beneath the actual bass-note. In this way, having the fundamental bass ever in view, we obtain a clearer insight into the leading of the voices.

SECTION XV.

The *position* of a chord in four-voiced harmony, is determined (*a*) by the intervals involved in the disposition of the upper three voices, or (*b*), by the tone which the Soprano sounds at the beginning of a harmonic phrase.

A. From the former consideration (*a*) we derive the following three positions :

1st.—A chord appears in *Close Position,* whenever its upper three voices lie so near to each other, that no tone belonging to that chord can be added, without doubling one of them.

2d.—A chord appears in *Open Position,* whenever a space is left between each two of the upper three voices, which might be occupied by a tone belonging to the chord.

3d.—In the case of a still wider space between each two of the three upper voices, the position is said to be *dispersed.*

B. The *Soprano* determines the following three positions :

1st.—A chord appears in the position of the *octave* (*Octave position*) if the soprano sounds the octave.

2d.—A chord appears in the position of the *third* (*Third position*) if the soprano sounds the third.

3d.—A chord appears in the position of the *fifth* (*Fifth position*) if the soprano sounds the fifth.

The position of the *first* chord of a harmonic phrase is a matter of choice, whilst that of the second and all other succeeding chords is subject to the laws of harmonic progression.

SECTION XVI.

The voices progress in the following modes :

1st.—Two voices progress in *parallel motion,* when they rise or fall at the same time.

2d.—They progress in *contrary motion,* if one voice rises while the other falls.

3d.—The *oblique motion* arises, if one voice remains on the same tone, while another is progressing.

The *parallel* motion requires a thorough discussion.

In the case of parallel motion of two voices, proceeding by degrees, the best progressions are, by thirds or sixths (*a*).

The parallel motion of three voices progressing by degrees, is best effected by letting the middle voice proceed by thirds and the upper by sixths, together with the lower voice (*b*) ; but it is of rather doubtful propriety when the middle voice proceeds by fourths and the upper by sixths to the lower voice (*c*). This lower voice in the four-voiced harmony, furthermore, cannot be the bass, as the latter in this case is obliged to move in contrary motion (*d*). The most objectionable progression would be, if an

upper voice were to move in fifths to a lower voice (*e*), or if any voice were
to move in fourths to the bass (*f*).

(a)

(b)   *(c)*

(d)

(e)   *(f)*

What has been said above concerning the progression by *degrees*, applies
also to that by *skips*.

Other objectionable progressions in parallel motion are *parallel primes*,
octaves and *fifths*.

Two voices move in *open primes*, if starting from the same degree, they
are found to be again perfect primes at the next progression, whether by
degrees or by skips, *e. g.*:

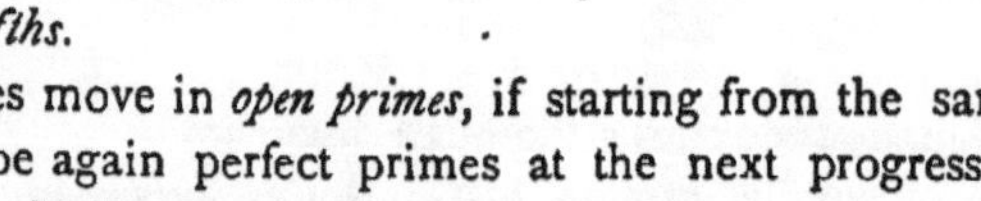

Two voices move in *covered primes*, if, beginning with any interval, **they
are** found in the next progression to be perfect primes, *e. g.*:

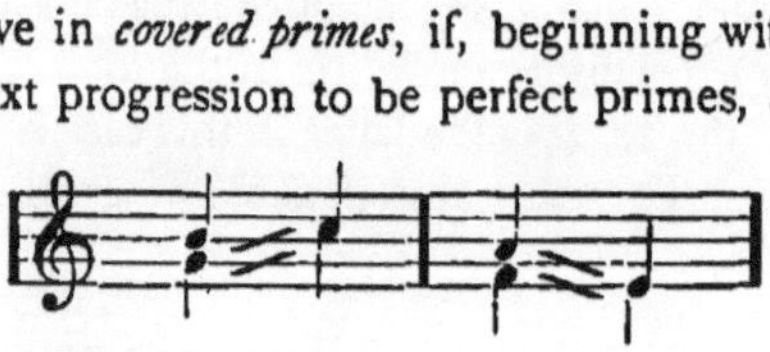

Two voices progress in *open octaves*, if they begin and end with a *perfect octave* (*a*), or in *covered octaves*, if they begin with *any interval*, to terminate with a *perfect octave* (*b*).

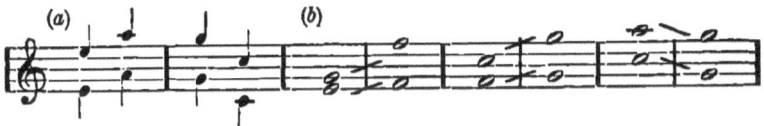

Two voices progress in *open fifths*, if they begin and end with a *perfect fifth* (*a*), or in *covered fifths*, if they begin with *any interval*, to terminate with a *perfect fifth* (*b*).

Two voices may progress in fifths, if the first fifth is *perfect*, and the second *diminished* (*a*), provided this does not occur in the outer voices (*b*).

Another objectionable progression occurs, when, of two tones forming a prime on the accented part of the measure, one skips away to form with the other a prime on the accented part of the next measure, *e. g.* :

NOTE.—The above rule and example might at first sight seem to apply only to *oblique*, rather than to *parallel* motion, with which we are now concerned. But examples of this kind, in which the skips occur on the *unaccented* part of the measure, belong more strictly to parallel than to oblique motion.

The same remarks apply to a similar progression in octaves (*a*) and in fifths (*b*), *e. g.* :

Of the above-named different kinds of motion, only the parallel motion in two or three voices can be applied by itself, due regard being had to the rules given above. But it oftener happens that a third or fourth voice pro- gresses in contrary motion, while at the same time still another remains on one degree, thereby producing the *oblique motion.* The best arrangement is, to let the bass ascend, while the other voices descend, and *vice versa.*

SECTION XVII.

During the continuance of the same fundamental, the component tones of its triad may exchange their positions. The most natural exchange is, when that voice which has the *octave* of the fundamental, skips to the *third,* while another, which has the *third,* skips to the *octave* (*a*).

The next best exchange is, when that voice which has the *third,* skips to the *fifth,* while another, which has the *fifth,* skips to the *third* (*b*).

One *octave* may ascend to the *third,* while another descends to the *fifth* (*c*).

Again, the *third* may descend to one *octave,* while the *fifth* ascends to another *octave* (*d*).

One *fifth* may ascend to the *octave,* while another may descend to the *third* (*e*).

The *octave* may descend to one *fifth,* while the *third* ascends to another *fifth* (*f*).

One *third* may skip to the *octave,* while another skips to the *fifth* (*g*).

The *octave* may ascend to one *third,* while the *fifth* descends to another *third* (*h*).

The *octave* may ascend to the *fifth,* while the *fifth* descends to the *octave* (*i*), and lastly:

The *fifth* may ascend to the *octave,* while the *octave* descends to the *fifth* (*h*).

These exchanges may be used singly, or combined, *e. g. :*

SECTION XVIII.

The exchanges may likewise be effected with the component tones of the chord of the seventh of the same fundamental, with the exception of the seventh itself, which admits of no exchange, unless it be the *dominant seventh*, which alone has that privilege, *e. g. :*

SECTION XIX.

In making the exchanges mentioned in Sections XVII and XVIII, intermediate tones, *not belonging to the chord,* may be inserted, as follows:

1st.—If in the skip to the third the intermediate tone is inserted, thus effecting two melodic steps, instead of a skip, such inserted tone is called a *passing tone, e. g.:*

2nd.—If in the skip to the fourth the two intermediate tones are inserted, thus effecting three melodic steps, instead of a skip, they are likewise called *passing tones, e. g.:*

The following are examples of these passing tones in four-voiced harmony:

The exchanges of the component tones of a chord of the seventh of the same fundamental, may also be effected by means of passing tones, if the rule laid down in Section XVIII is observed.

The application of *passing tones* during the continuance of the *dominant chord of the seventh,* with the respective *exchanges of the seventh* itself, may be seen in the following examples :

Without exchange of the seventh.

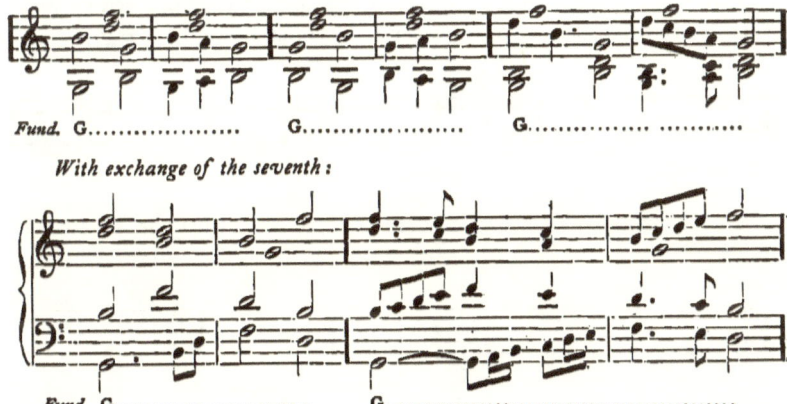

With exchange of the seventh:

The *essential tones* of the harmony must always appear upon the *accented part of the measure,* and must be of a duration either *equivalent to,* or *longer than that of the passing tones.*

The *passing chords* arising from the progression of the passing tones of the respective exchanges, must always be regarded as unessential harmonies.

A close scrutiny of the leading of the passing tones, will show that they succeed each other in strict conformity with the rules concerning parallel motion, as explained in Section XVI.

SECTION XX.

During the continuance of the same fundamental, each component tone of its triad may ascend or descend, immediately to return ; for instance :
In the triad of the 1st degree in the following manner :

In the dominant chord of the seventh :

Two voices progressing by this returning motion must proceed by *thirds* or *sixths in parallel motion,* or, *contrary motion* must be applied, *e. g.* :

A simultaneously returning motion of three voices may be effected as follows :

It is to be noticed in regard to these returning motions, that they pass to tones belonging to chords which bear a relation to the tonic triad, viz. : the chord of the seventh, and the chord of the seventh and ninth of the 5th degree, and to the triad of the 4th degree.

SECTION XXI.

During the continuance of the same fundamental, the octave in the triad may descend one degree, whereby a seventh, called a *passing seventh*, arises, while the remaining tones either maintain their position (*a*), or another octave skips to the third or fifth, the passing seventh requiring a resolution one degree downward (*b*).

The examples given at (*b*) are based on the same fundamental as at (*a*).

If the fundamental appears to ascend, at first a third and then a second, only two fundamentals occur in reality, viz. : the *first* and *last;* because the second bass note is obtained by the skip of one octave to its third ; and its fifth is obtained by the step of another octave to the passing seventh, which is amply illustrated by the last example, and by the following ones :

SECTION XXII.

Simultaneously with the step of one octave to the seventh, of the same fundamental, and the skip of another octave to the third, the third may also skip to the octave, by way of exchange, which, however, can be done without reserve upon the dominant only, as the free and simultaneous entrance of the fundamental and seventh of the other degrees would sound too harshly, *e. g.*:

Without exchange:

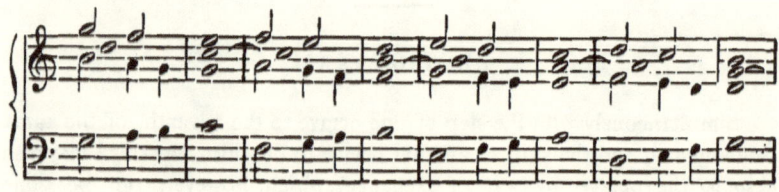

With exchange:

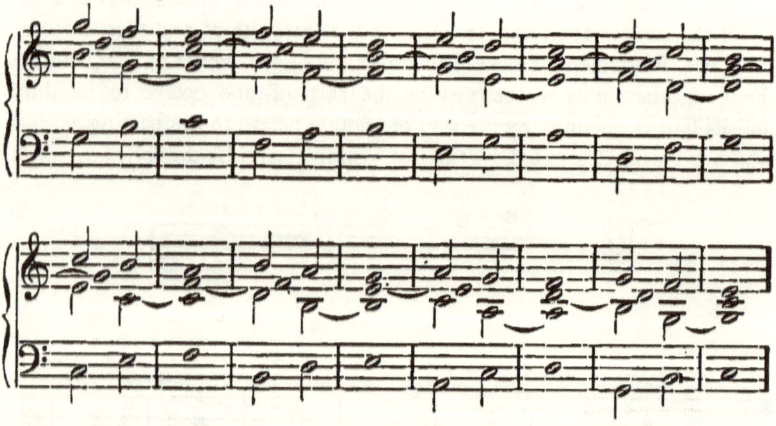

This harshness, however, may be easily avoided by allowing the entrance of the passing seventh to occur simultaneously with the passing tones of the exchanges, *e. g.*:

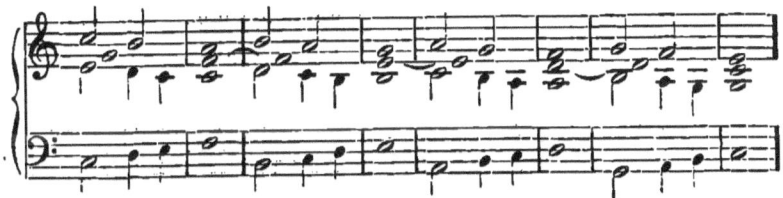

The 1st, 5th, 7th, 11th and 15th measures seem to contradict the principles laid down in Sec. XI ; but the correctness of the progression, nevertheless, becomes apparent, when we consider that the harmony of the third quarter of each of these measures occurs only accidentally, not necessarily.

If, simultaneously with the step of the octave to the passing seventh, and the entrance of the remaining passing tones, the *fifth descends* one degree, to return immediately, then care should be taken that the octave occur above the fifth, as in the following examples, at (*a*) and (*b*), since otherwise consecutive fifths would occur in parallel motion, as at (*c*).

SECTION XXIII.

Simultaneously with the step of the octave to the passing seventh, the *tenth·may step to the ninth* of the same fundamental. Special care should be taken, that the dubious fifth of the 2d, and the diminished fifth of the 7th degree occur above the ninth, since otherwise consecutive fifths would result (*a*).

(*a*)

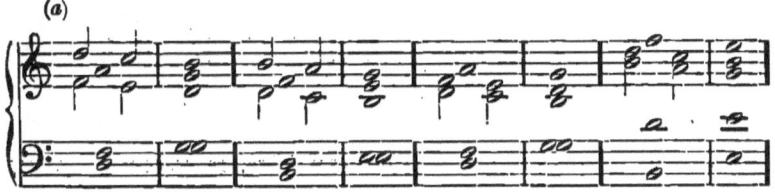

The perfect fifth may appear below or above the ninth, because it can either ascend or descend (*b*).

(*b*)

These progressions are usually effected in four-voiced harmony without the fundamental voice ; and in three-voiced harmony even without the lower third, *e. g.*:

SECTION XXIV.

If the fundamental descends a fifth, or ascends a fourth, the regular progressions of the tones take place in the following different ways :

1st.—The third of the first ascends one degree to the octave of the second fundamental (*a*) ; it ascends a fourth, or descends a fifth to the third of the second fundamental (*b*), or it remains as seventh of the second fundamental (*c*).

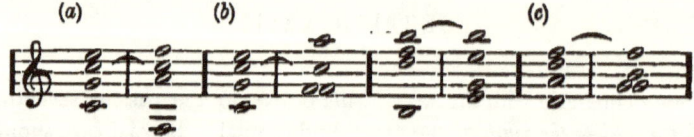

2d.—The octave may remain as fifth (*a*), or skip to the third (*b*), or to the octave, provided the bass remains, or progresses in contrary motion (*c*).

3d.—The fifth ascends one step to the third (*a*), or descends one step to the octave (*b*)

4th.—The seventh descends one degree to the third, *e. g.:*

SECTION XXV.

Although progressions involving covered fifths and octaves are usually prohibited, yet they cannot in all cases be avoided, unless the most natural progressions in harmony are also to be rejected. The following examples will elucidate the special exceptions to this rule :

A. *Covered fifths* are admissible :

(*a*). If the fundamental descends a fourth, while the third of the first descends one degree to the fifth of the second fundamental—

(*b*). If the fundamental ascends a fifth, while the octave of the first ascends one degree to the fifth of the second fundamental—

(*c*). If the third of the first fundamental ascends to the octave of the second, while the octave of the first fundamental ascends to the fifth of the second, *e. g.:*

The above exceptions, however, are subject to the following limitations :

1st.—They are not to be applied in two-voiced compositions, on account of the unsatisfactory effect produced by the absence of the third, but exclusively in compositions of three or more parts, affording the effect of full harmony.

2d.—The skipping voice must skip in reality, *i. e.,* without insertion of passing tones, *e. g.:*

(*d*). *Covered fifths* are admissible also, when the same chord is **inverted** into other positions, *e. g. :*

B.   Covered octaves are admissible :

(*a*). If the fundamental descends a fifth, while the fifth of the first descends one degree to the octave of the second fundamental.

(*b*). If the fundamental ascends a fourth, while the third of the first ascends one degree to the octave of the second fundamental, *e. g. :*

Provided, however, that this does not occur in two-voiced harmony, because of the unsatisfactory effect resulting from the absence of the third, but in compositions of three or more parts, affording the effect of full harmony: bearing in mind, as before, that the skipping voice must skip in reality, without insertion of passing tones, *e. g. :*

SECTION XXVI.

Conditions which are indispensable to a good four-voiced harmony, **are** the following :

1st.—Each voice must have a different progression from the others, which excludes octaves and fifths in parallel motion.

2d.—Whenever a primary chord is immediately succeeded by another, the two must be connected by a natural link, which with some chords produces a closer connection than with others.   This natural link is a perfect one, whenever the fifth is prepared, which may be effected by the descent of the fundamental by a fifth or third.   The ascent of the fundamental by a fifth or third, affords the preparation of the octave, which, however, in some instances leads to results which are objectionable.

3d.—In every harmonic phrase one voice, at least, should progress by melodic steps.

———

SECTION XXVII.

The most important chord is the *triad of the* 1*st degree*, which degree is also called *Tonic*, or *principal tone*, because every harmonic combination must bear relation to it, and because it forms the proper conclusion, as it is also the most appropriate commencement, of a composition.

The next important chord is the *triad*, or *chord of the seventh, of the* 5*th degree*, which degree is also called *Dominant*, inasmuch as it leads back directly to the tonic, and accordingly occurs as the last chord but one.

The *triad of the* 4*th degree*, which degree is called *subdominant*, is the third of the important chords, because it also affords the opportunity to return to the tonic triad.

Generally speaking, the tonic triad bears a direct relation to the dominant triad, or chord of the seventh, and to the subdominant triad, *e. g.*:

Degrees: I V I V̇ I IV I V̇ I, expressed by notes.

The next best progressions are those in which the fundamental descends by a fifth, or ascends by a fourth, (the result in both cases being the same), because the harmonic link is always perfect, and the change of harmony enters very distinctly; and finally, because the dissonances may be better prepared and resolved, *e. g.*:

I. Succession of triads formed upon fundamentals descending by a fifth.

II. Succession of chords of the seventh upon the same fundamental progression.

The expression, *regular progression of fundamentals*, implies a succession of *fundamental descents by a fifth.*

The descent of the fundamental by a third affords two links, the fifth and third, and is much weaker in its effect, because it introduces but a single new tone, *e. g.:*

SECTION XXVIII.

The progression from the chord of the seventh of the 5th to the triad of the 1st degree, is regarded as the most important. It serves as a model for many other progressions, and is called the *closing cadence.* It is effected in the following manner :

1st.—The voice having the fundamental tone of the chord of the seventh of the 5th degree, skips to the fundamental tone of the triad of the 1st degree, *i. e.*, it either descends by a fifth, or ascends by a fourth. This is therefore called a *fundamental progression.*

2d.—The voice having the seventh of the chord of the seventh of the 5th degree descends one degree to the third of the triad of the 1st degree. This is a *melodic progression.*

3d.—The voice having the third of the chord of the seventh of the 5th degree, ascends one degree to the octave of the fundamental of the triad of the 1st degree : this being also a melodic progression.

4th.—The voice having the fifth of the chord of the seventh of the 5th degree, descends best one degree to the octave, or ascends one degree to the third of the triad of the 1st degree ; both progressions being melodic.

5th.—The voice having the octave of the fundamental of the chord of the seventh of the 5th degree, remains, to become the 5th of the triad of the 1st degree, thereby forming the harmonic link between both chords.

The closing progression may also be made from the *triad* (instead of from the *chord of the seventh*) of the 5th to that of the 1st degree. This requires no other alteration than the omission of the seventh, and its substitution by the octave, which then descends by a third, or, the fifth of the 5th degree ascends one degree, in order to reach the third of the 1st degree, *e. g.:*

The same, with fewer voices:

In case a perfect close should not be intended, the third of the 5th degree may (instead of progressing to the octave) skip to the third of the 1st degree, *e. g* :

The same, with inversions :

Fund. G   C   G   C

Fund. G   C   G   C   G   C

SECTION XXIX.

The ascent of the fundamental by a fifth or a third, depends on the perfection or independence of both chords, in so far, that is, as the first chord requires no resolution, and the second no preparation. Hence the following perfect progressions remain, viz. :

A. *The ascent of the fundamental by a fifth :*
    1st.—From the 1st to the 5th degree ;
    2d.—From the 4th to the 1st degree ;
    3d.—From the 6th to the 3d degree.

B. *The ascent of the fundamental by a third :*
    1st.—From the 1st to the 3d degree ;
    2d.—From the 4th to the 6th degree ;
    3d.—From the 3d to the 5th degree :
    4th.—From the 6th to the 1st degree.

The ascent of fundamentals by a fifth or third, may be effected either *actually*, or by a *passing motion*, which latter, in some cases, is preferable to the former, as allowing the second chord to be succeeded by a more marked harmony than would otherwise be the case. The means of effecting this have been already elaborately discussed in Sections XVII—XXIII. Here follow a few examples :

From the 1st to the 3d degree.   *From the 6th to the 3d degree.*

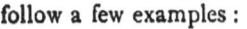

1. *By fundamental progression.*   2. *By passing motion.*   1. *By fundamental progression*   2. *By passing motion.*

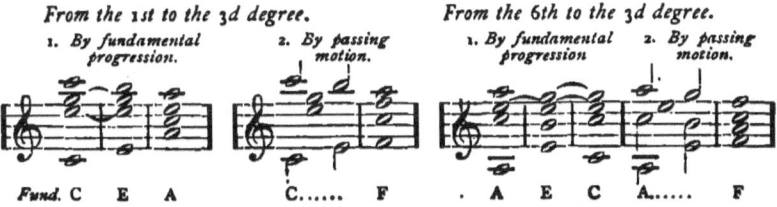

Fund. C   E   A   C......   F   A   E   C   A.....   F

SECTION XXX.

A succession of harmonies containing conditional tones, may be effected by means of passing motions, as follows :

1st.—The formation of the second chord may be effected upon the fundamental of the first chord (Sec. XXXI).

2d.—The fundamental tones of the two harmonies which are to follow each other, may be treated as component tones of a primary chord whose (inaudible) fundamental occurs a third lower than the lower of the two. (Sec. XXXII.)

3d.—The harmony of the second chord may be formed upon an assumed fundamental (Sec. XXXVII).

————

SECTION XXXI.

The second chord must be based upon the fundamental of the first, in the following instances :

1st.—If the triad of the 5th degree is to be succeeded by that of the 7th degree, which would be a fundamental ascent by a third :

2d.—If the triad of the 5th degree is to be succeeded by that of the 2d degree, which would be a fundamental ascent by a fifth :

3d.—If the triad of the 2d degree is to be succeeded by the harmony of the 4th degree, which is a fundamental ascent by a third ; and,

4th.—If the triad of the 2d degree is to be succeeded by the harmony of the 6th degree, which would be a fundamental ascent by a fifth.

The triad of the 5th degree cannot be succeeded by the diminished triad of the 7th degree, by way of fundamental progression, because the diminished fifth is not prepared ; nevertheless, this succession may be effected by means of a passing motion, upon the fundamental of the 5th degree, if one octave skips to the third or fifth, while another descends to the seventh, *e. g.* :

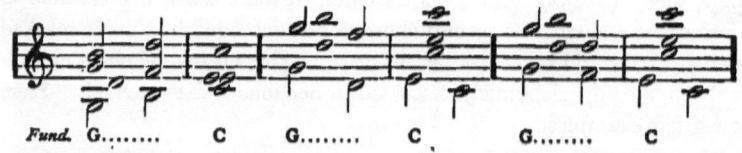

The triad of the 5th degree cannot be succeeded by the harmony of the 2d degree, by fundamental progression, because the dubious fifth of the 2d degree is not prepared, but this harmony may be obtained upon the fundamental of the 5th degree, if one octave descends to the seventh, at the same time that

another octave ascends one degree, to descend again simultaneously with
the descent of a returning step of the third, *e. g. :*

Fund. G............ C........ G............ C

The triad of the 2d degree cannot be succeeded by the harmony of the
4th degree, by fundamental progression, because the dubious fifth of the
2d degree would thereby lose its dubious character, by remaining as third
of the 4th degree, in which character it might ascend. But this succession
may be based upon the fundamental of the 2d degree, if one octave of the
fundamental ascends to its third, while another descends to the seventh,
e. g. :

Fund. D....... G C D........ G C D...... G C

The triad of the 2d degree cannot be succeeded by the harmony of the
6th degree, by way of fundamental progression, because the dubious fifth
of the 2d degree would lose its dubious character by remaining as perfect
octave of the 6th degree : still, this connection may be effected upon the
fundamental of the 2d degree, if one octave descends to the seventh, simultaneously with the descent of the tenth to the ninth, while at the same
time another octave skips to the fifth, *e. g. :*

Fund. D............ G C D.......... G..... C D......... G C

SECTION XXXII.

The diminished triad of the 7th degree cannot be succeeded by the harmony of the 2d degree, by way of fundamental progression, because the
diminished fifth of the 7th degree cannot become a consonance by remaining as third of the 2d degree, and because the dubious fifth of the 2d degree
is not prepared. This succession, however, can be obtained, if the funda-

mental tones of the 7th and 2d degrees (*b and d*) throw off their fundamental character, and stand instead as component tones of a primary chord, the fundamental of which would be found a third below the lower of the two (*g*). In this way, the required progression may be satisfactorily obtained by means of the several passing motions, *e. g.:*

The diminished triad of the 7th degree cannot be succeeded by the harmony of the 4th degree, by way of fundamental progression, because the diminished fifth of the 7th degree cannot become a consonance by remaining as octave of the 4th degree. This succession, however, can be obtained if the fundamental tones of the 7th and 4th degrees (*b and f*) throw off their fundamental character, and stand instead as component tones of a primary chord, the fundamental of which would be found a third below the lower of the two (*g*). In this case the required succession may be satisfactorily obtained by means of the several passing motions, *e. g.:*

It should be observed here that by means of the passing motions just explained, inversions of chords of the seventh may be introduced freely : provided, however, that at least one tone of these inversions exist in the preceding chord, that the tones reached by skips are component parts of the fundamental harmony, whilst other tones, especially that which represents the seventh, may be reached by melodic steps, and that unprepared sevenths, ninths and seconds are avoided, *e. g.:*

SECTION XXXIII.

A direct, regular progression of fundamentals by degrees, does not exist, since their harmonies are without any natural link. But this progression may be effected by the introduction of a *tacit fundamental*, which should be a fifth above the second actual fundamental, thereby affording the desired natural link.

Here follow examples of fundamentals ascending by degrees :

Fund. C A   D   F D   G   B G   C   D B   E

More correctly thus :

It is obvious, that, with the seeming ascent of the fundamental by degrees, the first harmony *undergoes a change* by the insertion of the *tacit fundamental.* The first *triad* is changed into a *chord of the seventh* of a tacit fundamental, or, in other words, the triad of the first fundamental stands as substitute for a chord of the seventh, the resolution of which leads to the desired harmony of the second (actual) fundamental.

SECTION XXXIV.

Irregular progressions of the voices may occur under the following restrictions :

1st.—The *seventh* may *ascend* one degree, a license which can never occur in the bass, and is admitted in the other voices only under the following conditions, viz. : (*a*) That the fundamental is not audible, so that the seventh does not appear as such : (*b*) That another voice (most generally the bass) effects the resolution of the seventh ; and (*c*) That such a position is chosen, as enables the ascending third of the first (*tacit*) fundamental to stand above the irregular ascending seventh, so as to prevent any succession of fifths, which would otherwise result, *e.g.* :

Faulty.

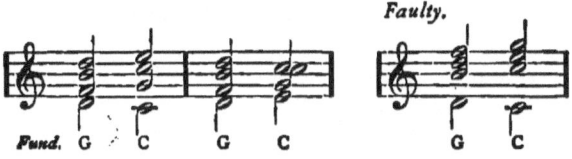

Fund. G   C   G   C   G   C

Under the above-named conditions, two sevenths, one descending, and the other ascending, may occur simultaneously, *e. g.*:

Fund. C A D   C A D   C A D

2d.—The third, instead of ascending to the octave, remaining as seventh, or skipping to the third of the second fundamental (all of which are regular progressions), may skip to the fifth of the second fundamental, either by descending a third, or by ascending a sixth. This license also cannot be extended to the bass, and is admitted in the other voices only on the following conditions : (*a*) the skip from the third of the first to the fifth of the second fundamental, if it descends a third, must occur in a lower voice than that in which the regular progression of the fundamental descent, or the regular progression of the fifth of the first to the octave of the second fundamental takes place, since otherwise consecutive fifths would arise, *e. g.*:

Fund. G   C   G   C   G   C

(*b*). For the same reason, namely, to avoid covered fifths, the skip from the third of the first to the fifth of the second fundamental, if it ascends a sixth, must appear in a lower voice than that in which the regular ascending progression of the fundamental by a fourth, or the regular progression of the third of the first to the octave of the second fundamental occurs, *e. g.*:

Fund. C   F   C   F   C   F

3d.—The fifth, instead of ascending one degree to the third, or descending one degree to the octave of the second fundamental, may ascend or descend to the fifth of the second fundamental. This license is also denied to the bass, and is granted to the other voices under the following restrictions, viz. :

(*a*). The skip of the fifth of the first, to the fifth of the second fundamental, whenever it descends a fifth, must occur in a lower voice than that in which the regular fundamental descent by a fifth, or the regular progres-

sion of the fifth of the first to the octave of the second fundamental occurs,
e. g.:

(*b.*) The skip from the fifth of the first to the fifth of the second fundamental, if it ascends a fourth, must be made in a lower voice than that which effects the regular progression of the fundamental ascent by a fourth, and than that which effects the regular progression of the third to the octave of the second fundamental, otherwise consecutive fifths occur, *e. g.:*

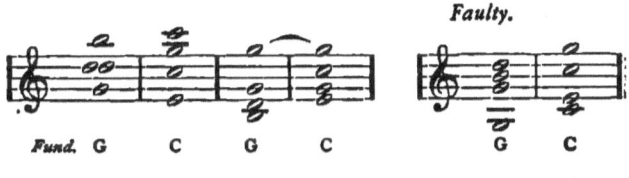

SECTION XXXV.

The *descent* of the fundamentals by degrees depends likewise upon the insertion of a *tacit fundamental*, which should form a fundamental descent by a fifth to the second actual fundamental. The triad of the first (*actual*) fundamental will then stand as substitute for a chord of the seventh and ninth, the resolution of which effects the desired harmony of the second (actual) fundamental (*a*). The position of the first triad must be so chosen, that that fifth which is to be changed into a ninth, does not appear in the soprano, as consecutive fifths would arise (*b*), nor in the bass, as parallel fourths would occur against the bass (*c*), This leaves as bass note of the first triad its fundamental only, which would stand as fifth (*d*), or its third, which would stand as seventh (*e*) of the tacit fundamental. It is apparent, that the triad of the first actual fundamental can be succeeded only by the first inversion of the triad of the second actual fundamental, if the latter descends one degree.

(*b*) *Faulty.*   (*c*) *Faulty.*

Fund. D G C   D G C   D G C   D G C

(*d*)   (*e*)

Fund. D G C   D G C

Exceptions to this occur, if the triad of the 4th is to be succeeded by the harmony of the 3d degree, that of the 6th by the harmony of the 5th degree, and that of the 1st by the harmony of the 7th degree.

1st.—If the triad of the 6th degree is to be succeeded by the harmony of the 5th, through the medium of the actual or tacit fundamental of the 2d degree, the bass note of the first triad is changed into a dubious fifth of the 2d degree, which must *descend one* degree, as the progression of the bass admits no licenses. The *octave* of the triad (another dubious fifth) must *ascend*, otherwise consecutive octaves would arise; and this it may do, because its resolution is effected by the bass.

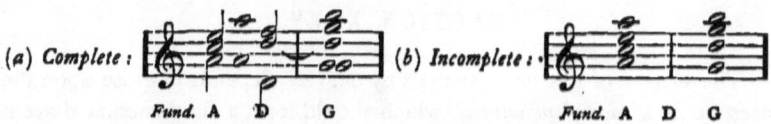

(*a*) *Complete :*   (*b*) *Incomplete :*

Fund. A   D   G   Fund. A   D   G

This last example (*b*) contains three licences: the ascent of the dubious fifth, of the seventh, and of the ninth, which, however, may be easily explained according to Section XXXIV.

2d.—A similar progression must be applied in the case of the succession of the triads of the 4th and 3d degrees, *e. g.* :

(*a*) *Complete.*   (*b*) *Incomplete.*

Fund. F B E

A fundamental progression from the 6th to the 5th, and from the 4th to the 3d degrees, may also be effected three-voiced, if, instead of the triad of the 6th or 4th degree, their 1st inversion is employed.

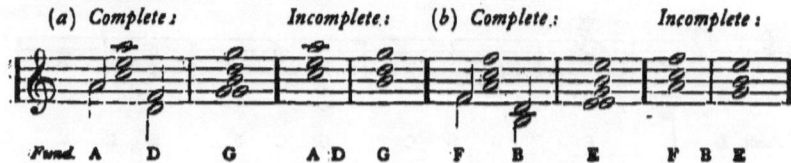

(*a*) *Complete :*   *Incomplete :*   (*b*) *Complete :*   *Incomplete :*

Fund. A   D   G   A D G   F   B   E   F B E

SECTION XXXVI.

Since the seventh of the dominant chord of the seventh requires no preparation, this chord and all its inversions have great freedom in their progressions. They may enter free after the following chords :

1st.—After the *tonic triad* and its inversions.

2d.—After the *dominant triad* and its inversions.

3d.—After the *triad of the 3d degree.* But the *first inversion* of this triad cannot be followed by the *second inversion* of the dominant chord of the seventh. The *second inversion* of this triad (chord of the fourth and sixth) can be succeeded only by the *first inversion* of the dominant chord of the seventh, the chord of the fifth and sixth.

After all the chords which would prepare the dominant seventh, the seventh may appear in another voice than that in which it previously occurred, excepting such voice as has to resolve a dissonance.

It should be observed, however, that after the *triad of the 6th degree*, the dominant chord of the seventh enters abruptly, inasmuch as these two chords have no common tone to form a connecting link.

SECTION XXXVII.

The *tonic triad* cannot be succeeded by the *triad of the 7th degree* in direct fundamental progression, because the diminished fifth of the latter is not prepared ; but the succession may be effected seemingly, if the triad of the 7th degree is introduced as substitute for the dominant chord of the seventh, that is, without fundamental, *e. g.* :

The diminished triad of the 7th degree may stand as substitute for the dominant chord of the seventh, not only after the tonic triad (*a*), but also after the triad of the 5th (*b*), and that of the 3d degree (*c*), which progressions are particularly adapted to three-voiced harmony, *e. g.* :

In free harmony the dominant ninth may enter unprepared, if it appears in the upper voice, *e. g.* :

This is all the more allowable if the dominant chord of the seventh and ninth appears without its fundamental, *i. e.*, when its substitute (the chord of the seventh of the 7th degree, or one of its inversions) takes its place, *e. g.* :

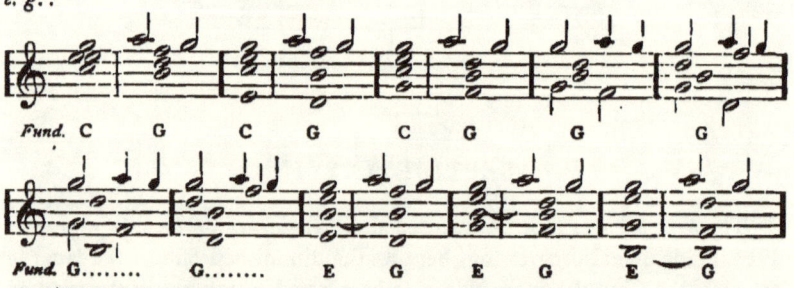

Additional examples will be given with the *suspensions*.

SECTION XXXVIII.

In Section XXVIII, allusion was made to the progression from the dominant triad, or the chord of the seventh, to the tonic triad, which we termed the *closing cadence* (authentic close), and which we shall now fully discuss.

The formation of a perfect closing cadence depends upon the contraction of all the diatonic tones of the scale, and is effected by the succession of the triads of the 4th, 5th and 1st degrees, or by the succession of the triads, or chords of the seventh, of the 2d and 5th, and the triad of the 1st degree (*a*).

Other cadences (still more contracted) arise, if the harmony of the 6th is succeeded by that of the 5th degree (*b*), and the harmony of the 3d by that of the 5th degree (*c*); but they have not the decisive character of the former ones, *e. g.* :

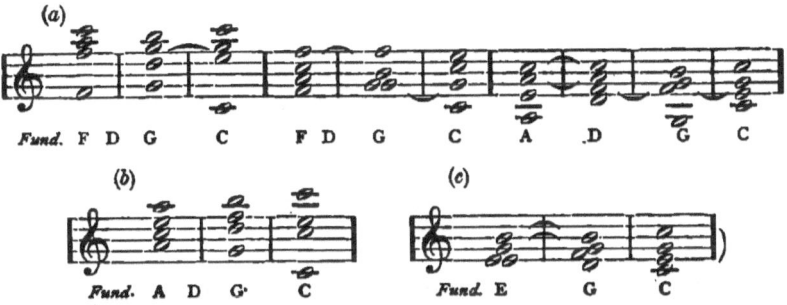

The *plagal close* (succession of the triads of the 4th and 1st degrees), seldom stands alone, being preceded most generally by the *authentic* close.

SECTION XXXIX.

The succession of the harmonies of the 4th, 5th and 1st degrees, and of the 2d, 5th and 1st degrees, as explained in the foregoing Section, invest the third of the 5th degree with an unmistakable tendency to resolve itself into the octave of the 1st degree, in consequence of which, it is called *leading tone*. This tendency of the leading tone forbids its duplication (as involving octaves or primes), and also its skipping away to any other tone.

SECTION XL.

In contradistinction to the progression of the component tones of a chord simultaneously with the entrance of a new fundamental, it may happen that one voice does not resolve, as expected, but continues as a foreign tone in the new harmony, and resolves at a subsequent period.   In such a case we have a *suspension*.

A suspension may occur in any voice, and every tone of a triad, or chord of the seventh, may be suspended in the following manner :

1st.—If the fundamental descends by a fifth, or ascends by a fourth, (which gives the same result), and the first chord is a chord of the seventh, the fifth and seventh must descend one degree.   By their suspension at the entrance of the new fundamental, the seventh is changed into an *eleventh*, and the fifth into a *ninth*, both of which must afterwards resolve into the *tenth* and *octave*.   Accordingly the *eleventh* stands as a suspension of the *third* from above, and is accompanied by the *octave* and *fifth* of the fundamental ; and the *ninth* as a suspension of the *octave* from above, and is accompanied by the *third* and *fifth*.

The names *eleventh* and *ninth* are adopted for the reason that the *eleventh* must form a ninth above that voice which sounds the third, and the *ninth* a ninth above that voice which sounds the octave ; because a tone can never lie close to or above its suspension, *e. g.* :

The examples show the disposition of the voices, (*a*) when the suspensions occur accompanied by their suspension-tones ; (*b*) when they occur alone.

2d.—If the fundamental descends by a fourth, or ascends by a fifth (which gives the same result), and both chords are triads, the *octave* and the *third* must descend one degree, but their suspension changes them, at the entrance of the new fundamental, the *former* into an *eleventh*, and the *latter* into a *thirteenth*, both of which must afterwards resolve into the *tenth* and *twelfth*.   The thirteenth, therefore, stands as suspension of the fifth from above, and is accompanied by the third and octave.   Here the term *thirteenth* is adopted, for the reason that the *thirteenth* must form a *ninth* above that voice which sounds a fifth, *e. g.* :

The examples show the disposition of the voices, (*a*) when the suspensions occur unaccompanied by their suspension-tones; (*b*) when they occur accompanied by them.

The following examples show the use of suspensions in inverted chords, and moreover, some faulty leading of the voices.

It should here also be noticed, that the ninth, eleventh and thirteenth, should not be mistaken for the second, fourth and sixth ; the former being tones foreign to the harmony, admitting of no duplication ; while the latter are component parts of the harmony, and may be doubled.

It should be observed, furthermore, that the suspensions do not remove parallel fifths or octaves, as the following examples will show :

1st.—Suspensions of the Ninth.

If the suspension of the ninth occurs in the bass, the octave of the fundamental cannot appear in a higher voice, for the reasons given above.

2d.—SUSPENSIONS OF THE ELEVENTH.

The first inversion of the chord of the eleventh can follow only after the first inversion of the preceding triad, *e. g.*:

If the eleventh occurs in the bass, the third of the fundamental cannot appear in a higher voice, for the reasons given above.

3d.—SUSPENSIONS OF THE THIRTEENTH.

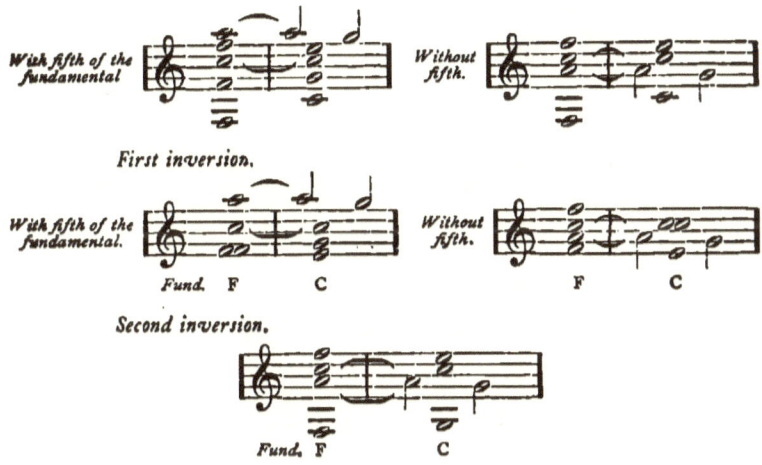

With fifth of the fundamental / Without fifth.

First inversion.

With fifth of the fundamental. / Without fifth.

Fund. F   C   F   C

Second inversion.

Fund. F   C

Here follows the suspension of the thirteenth in the bass, with inversion of the triad (*a*), and inversion of the chord of the seventh (*b*).

Fund. F   C   C   C   G   C

The *ascending seventh.* If the triad of the 5th is succeeded by that of the 1st degree, the third of the former ought to resolve into the octave of the latter. If the resolution of the third is delayed, the major third of the 5th remains as major seventh of the 1st degree, and stands as suspension of the octave from below, into which it must be resolved. The same rules hold good here as with the suspensions from above, viz. : that a suspension tone can never lie close to its suspension, nor above it. The same suspension may occur if the triad of the 1st is succeeded by that of the 4th degree.

Faulty.   Good.

First inversion.

With octave of the fundamental. / Without octave.

Fund. G   C   G   C

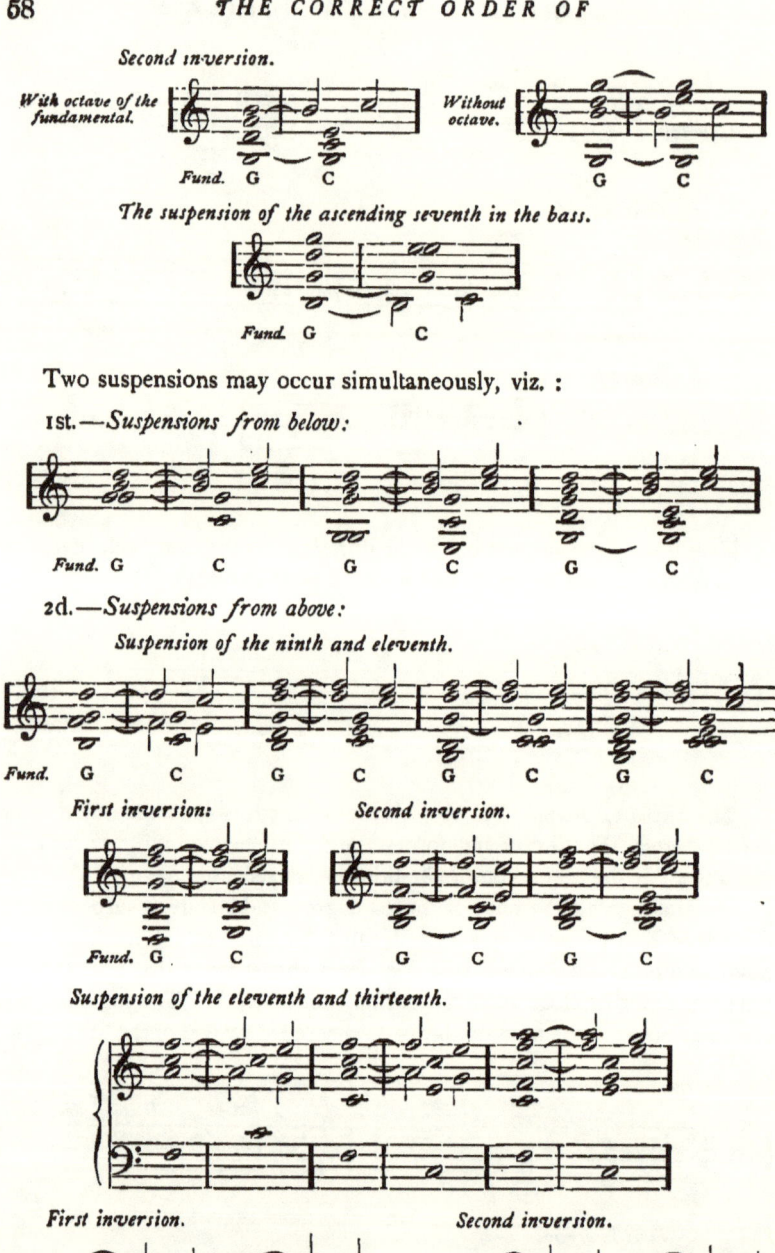

Two suspensions may occur simultaneously, viz. :

1st.—*Suspensions from below:*

2d.—*Suspensions from above:*

Three suspensions may occur simultaneously, viz. : those of the eleventh, ninth, and ascending seventh, *e. g.:*

The first inversion of the foregoing suspensions can follow only after the chord of the third and fourth, *e. g.:*

If the fundamental ascends a fourth, and the second chord is a chord of the seventh, the delay of the resolution of the fifth of the first chord changes the same into a ninth, whereby the sound of the third, fifth, seventh and ninth is obtained, which latter must then resolve into the octave, *e. g.:*

It may be observed here, that the ninth possesses merely a fictitious independence, since it is only a suspension of the octave, although the simultaneous sound of the fundamental, third, fifth, seventh and ninth, is called a chord of the seventh and ninth.

When the dominant chord of the seventh and ninth occurs without fundamental, the chord of the seventh of the 7th degree appears to be succeeded by the first inversion of the dominant chord of the seventh ; hence an opportunity is given for the descent of the fundamental by a third after every chord of the seventh, by which descent the seventh, fifth, third and fundamental are changed into the ninth, seventh, fifth and third of the new fundamental. The subsequent resolution of the ninth effects then a new chord of the seventh, *e. g.:*

If the second chord of the last example occurs without fundamental, the harmony of the dominant chord of the seventh is succeeded by that of the chord of the seventh of the 3d degree. The progression of the fundamentals in this case may be termed *artificial*, because both chords cannot be primary chords.

———

SECTION XLI.

The resolution of the ninth, instead of taking place during the continuance of the same fundamental, may be effected simultaneously with the entrance of the new fundamental, when it leads into the fifth.

Two fundamental progressions are necessary : the first, *to introduce the ninth* as suspension of the octave ; and the second, *to resolve the ninth* (of the second) into the fifth (of the third fundamental).

Without suspension.   *Suspension of the ninth.*   *Delayed resolution of the ninth.*

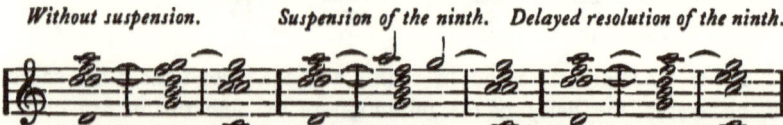

In cases like those just exemplified, it is necessary that the dubious fifth of the 2d, and the diminished fifth of the 7th degree should stand above the ninth, since otherwise consecutive fifths would arise ; while a perfect fifth may stand above or below the ninth, because it can ascend or descend, according to the necessity of the case.

From this resolution of the ninth into the fifth of the succeeding fundamental, arise seeming progressions of the fundamental, ascending by degrees from the chord of the seventh of the first fundamental to a triad or chord of the seventh of the second fundamental, *e. g. :*

(a) *Complete.*   (b) *Incomplete.*

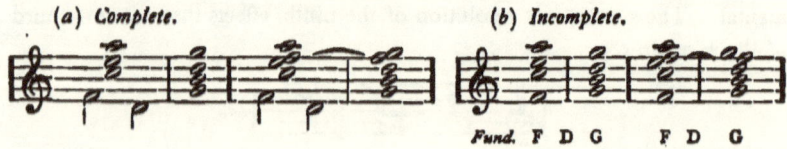

Fund. F D G   F D G

SECTION XLII.

The resolution of the ninth may be delayed still longer, if, instead of proceeding to the fifth, simultaneously with the entrance of the new fundamental, it remains suspended as thirteenth, to descend afterwards to the twelfth (fifth), *e. g.*

The last example exhibits the dominant chord of the seventh and ninth with a tacit fundamental. It seems, therefore, as if the chord of the seventh, of the 7th degree, were succeeded by the first inversion of the triad of the 6th degree before the tonic triad is heard ; but it will be seen, upon reflection, that *b* is *third*, and *c*, instead of being third, is *fundamental*.

Simultaneously with the delay of the resolution of the ninth, the resolution of the seventh may also be delayed, provided the fundamentals progress as in the last examples, *e. g.* :

It may be mentioned here, that by means of this protracted delay of the resolution of the ninth, and the simultaneous suspension of three more tones, all the diatonic tones of the major scale may sound simultaneously, *e. g.* :

In free harmony it is allowed to insert other tones between a suspension and its resolution. The tones thus inserted may be either component parts of the harmony (*a*), or foreign to it (*b*), in which latter case they are called *changing tones, e. g.* :

SECTION XLIII.

In regard to the nature of the chord of the dominant seventh, we may add, as a supplement to Section XXXVI, that the *octave* (of the fundamental) may proceed to the *seventh*, while the *thirteenth* resolves into the *fifth, e. g.:*

The last examples seem to indicate, at the commencement of each second measure, the harmony of the third degree: an observing mind, however, will easily distinguish the essential from the accidental harmony. In regard to the progression from the actual harmony of the third degree to the seeming diminished harmony of the 7th degree, (as explained in Section XXXVII), it may also be mentioned, that the harmony of the 3d degree can be taken as *apparent* only, if considered as suspended, *e. g.:*

The above observation applies equally to the chord of the dominant seventh and ninth, *e. g.:*

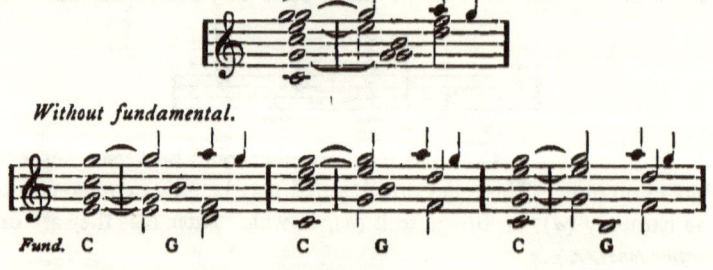

SECTION XLIV.

Some supplementary remarks must now be made with regard to *passing motions*. Those already explained in Sections XVII—XXIII, were all effected during the continuance of the same fundamental, whence they are called *regular*. On the other hand, passing motions are *irregular*, when effected simultaneously with the entrance of a new fundamental, *e. g.:*

Irregular passing motions may be introduced, as follows :

1st.—The octave, instead of progressing to the seventh during the continuance of the same fundamental, may effect this step simultaneously with the entrance of the next fundamental, when it will appear as *free eleventh*, which must resolve into the *tenth* (third).

2d.—The tenth, instead of progressing to the ninth during the continuance of the same fundamental, may effect this step simultaneously with the entrance of the next fundamental, when it will appear as *thirteenth*, which must resolve into the *twelfth* (fifth), *e. g.*

NOTE.—In cases like the above, care should be taken that the *bass* progresses in *contrary motion*.

SECTION XLV.

The suspension enters always upon the *accented part of the measure* (thesis), whether the preparation was effected on the *unaccented* part of the measure (arsis) or not ; it should be of no longer duration than its preparation, and not of shorter duration than its tone of resolution. This, however, does not imply that the tone of resolution may not serve again as preparation for another suspension, *e. g.* :

SECTION XLVI.

The contrary of the suspension is the *anticipation*, i. e., a *premature reso-lution*.

The tone of anticipation should always be so placed as not to lie close to another voice which is to resolve into the same tone (already sounded by the anticipation), otherwise the regular progression of the voice lying close to the anticipation would be hindered, *e. g.*:

It is well to have the tone of anticipation quite short in proportion to the tone preceding it, *e. g.*:

SUPPLEMENTARY REMARKS.

The general principles thus far laid down, should be applied according to the directions which here follow :

I. The triad of each degree of the major scale should, whenever it is practicable, be followed severally by the triad of every other degree, and the harmonic succession should be continued—by the descent of the fundamental by a fifth, by its ascent by a fourth, or its descent by a third—until a closing cadence is effected.

II. The same triad should, whenever it is practicable, be succeeded by the first inversion of the triad of every other degree, and be continued until a close is reached.

III. The same triad should, whenever it is practicable, be succeeded by the second inversion of the triad of every other degree, and be continued until a close is reached.

IV. The same triad should, whenever it is practicable, be succeeded by the chord of the seventh of every other degree, and be continued until a close is reached.

V. The same triad should, whenever it is practicable, be succeeded by the first inversion of the chord of the seventh of every other degree, and be continued until a close is reached.

VI. The same triad should, whenever it is practicable, be succeeded by the second inversion of the chord of the seventh of every other degree, and be continued until a close is reached.

VII. The same triad should, whenever it is practicable, be succeeded by the third inversion of the chord of the seventh of every other degree, and be continued until we arrive at a close.

In like manner, it is well that the chord of the seventh of each degree be succeeded by the triad, and the chord of the seventh, of each degree, with their respective inversions.

Thus, also, every individual inversion of the triads and chords of the seventh of all degrees, should be considered as starting-point, in order to ascertain whether they can be succeeded by the primary chords (with inversions) of the various other degrees.

It should be observed, furthermore, that these harmonic progressions may be effected either in close or in open position, by means of three, four or more voices, and should be transposed into all the different major scales.

As regards these exercises, it is to be observed, that the leading of the voices must be effected according to the directions given in Sections **XXIV** and XXVI, in other words, that the progressions of the upper voices should contain as few skips as possible. The leading of the bass, however, should be such as not only to avoid the moving about within a few tones, but also to form a free and melodious progression, which may be effected by a judicious alternation of primary and inverted chords. It is further advisable, that the student should lead the bass as much as possible in contrary motion to the other voices.

For further guidance with regard to the order of exercises, the following table will be found of service, in addition to which, we shall simply state, that the Roman ciphers indicate the harmony of that degree which serves as starting-point, while the Arabic figures indicate those degrees whose respective harmonies are to be connected with the harmony of the starting-point.

Each primary chord and its inversion of the 1st degree, should be succeeded alternately by the primary chords and inversions of the 5th, 4th, 6th, 3d, 2d, and 7th degrees.

$$V: 1, 3, 6, 4, 7, 2.$$
$$II: 5, 7, 3, 1, 4, 6.$$
$$VI: 2, 4, 1, 5, 3, 7.$$
$$III: 6, 1, 5, 4, 2, 7.$$
$$VII: 3, 5, 1, 6, 2, 4.$$
$$IV: 7, 2, 6, 5, 1, 3.$$

Here follow, as an illustration of the above, the harmonic successions of the harmony of the 7th degree of the major scale.

HARMONIC SUCCESSIONS OF THE TRIAD OF THE 7TH DEGREE.

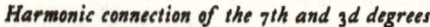

Harmonic connection of the 7th and 3d degrees.

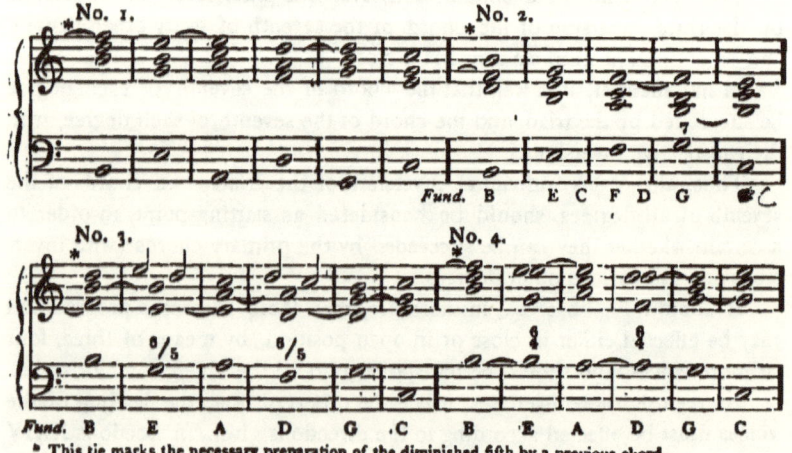

* This tie marks the necessary preparation of the diminished fifth by a previous chord.

The triad of the 7th degree cannot be succeeded by the third inversion of the chord of the seventh of the 3d degree, because the bass of the latter is not prepared.

REMARKS.—No. 1 contains two licences : (*a*) the ascent of the dubious fifth of the 2d degree, and (*b*) the skip of the leading tone to the fifth of the next fundamental (See Section XXXIX). No. 2 illustrates the repeated succession of fundamentals, ascending by degrees (Sec. XXXIII). No. 3 illustrates the descent of one octave (of the fundamental) to the passing seventh (Sec. XXI). No. 5 contains one license, viz. : the ascent of the diminished fifth of the 7th degree, which is admissible, since its resolution is effected by the bass. No. 7 illustrates the descent of fundamentals by degrees, and contains three licenses, viz.: the ascent of the dubious fifth, of the seventh, and of the ninth, of the 2d degree. (See Section XXXIV.)

The first example shows a symmetrical repetition of the 1st and 2d measures in the 3d and 4th, and in the 5th and 6th measures. This symmetrical repetition is called *Sequence*. Thus, the 3d, 4th and 6th examples exhibit a *sequence* in the 1st and 2d, and in the 3d and 4th measures, while in the 5th example it occurs in the 2d and 3d, and in the 4th and 5th measures.

Harmonic connections of the 7th and 1st degrees.

The diminished triad of the 7th degree cannot be succeeded by the 2d inversion of the tonic triad (See Sec. XI, 3).

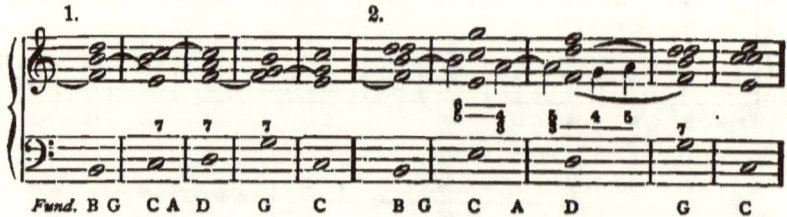

The 2d measure of the last example illustrates the artificial progression of fundamentals, as explained in Sec. XL, and a returning motion of the dubious fifth of the 2d degree in the third measure, the dubious fifth ascending to the leading tone ; which is a license.

The second inversion of the chord of the seventh of the 1st degree, cannot follow after the diminished triad of the 7th degree (Sec. XII).

The third inversion, however, may follow that triad.

The harmonic connection of the 7th and 6th degrees can be effected by means of the following progressions :

The harmonic connection of the 7th and 2d degrees may be effected by means of the passing motions only (Sec. XXXII).

Fund. G.............. C G............. C

The diminished triad of the 7th degree cannot be succeeded by the chord of the seventh of the 2d degree (Sec. XII), nor by its first inversion (Sect. XXXII).

The harmonic connection of the 7th and 4th degrees can be effected only by means of passing motion (Sec. XXXII).

No. 1.   No. 2.   No. 3.   No. 4.   No. 5.

Fund. G........ C G...... C G....... C G...... C G......... C

REMARKS.—The progression in the 1st example is effected by means of the skip of the third (of the tacit fundamental) to the seventh, a license which is admitted only upon the fundamental of the dominant. The progressions in the 2d and 3d examples are preferable to those in the 1st, because the succession is effected by means of the returning motion and melodic connection of the exchanges, and because the duplication of the seventh is avoided. The diminished triad of the 7th degree cannot be succeeded by the chord of the seventh of the 4th degree.

The succession of the diminished triad of the 7th and harmony of the 5th degree must be effected by means of a passing motion, the former being treated as substitute for the dominant chord of the seventh.

No. 1.   No. 2.   No. 3.   No. 4.

Fund. G...... C G C G...... C G...... C

Nos. 1 and 2 need no particular explanation; but No. 3 contains two licenses, viz.: the skipping away of the leading tone, and the free entrance of a fourth in the outer voices, which is prohibited in all the other harmonic progressions, and tolerated only upon the fundamental of the 5th degree. The same license occurs in the 6th example; but with this difference, that it occurs there in the tenor, and does not appear with the same prominence. The 7th example also contains two licenses, viz.: the skip of the third (of the tacit fundamental) to the seventh, and the skip of the fifth to the octave, from which the free entrance of a second results, which is also a license exclusively appertaining to the dominant harmony.

THE HARMONIC SUCCESSIONS OF THE FIRST INVERSION OF THE DIMINISHED TRIAD OF THE 7TH DEGREE.

VII. I.

Fund. B G C   B G C

The last example contains one license, viz. : the irregular progression from the fifth of the first to the fifth of the second fundamental. See Section XXXIV, 3.

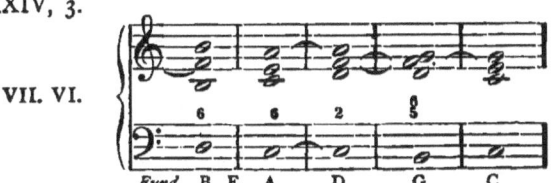

VII. VI.

Fund. B E A   D   G   C

VII. II.—*By means of passing motions.*

Fund. G............ C G.... ...... C G............. C

Fund. G....... .... C G............. C G........... C......

VII. IV.—*By means of passing motions.*

Fund. G............... C G............... C

Fund. G................ C........ G............... C

VII. V.—*By means of passing motions.*

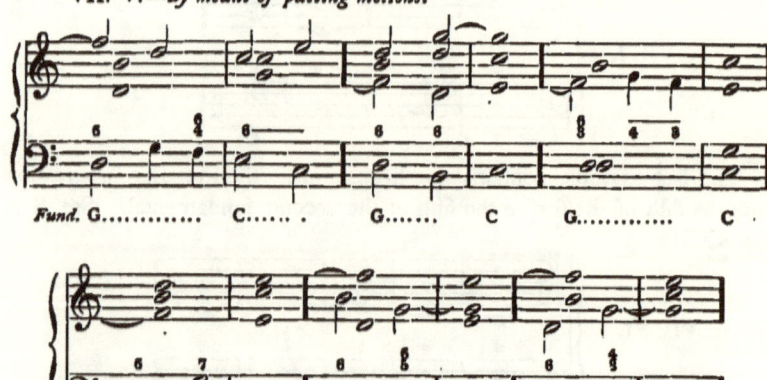

The Harmonic Successions of the Second Inversion of the Diminished Triad of the 7th Degree.

VII. III.

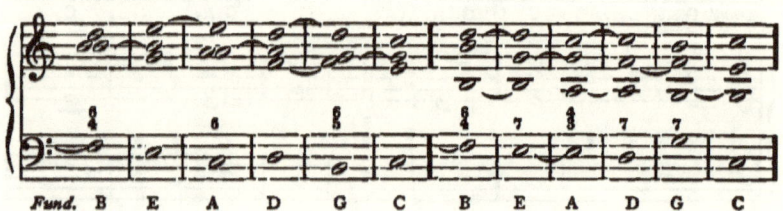

The second inversion of the diminished triad of the 7th degree cannot be succeeded by an inversion either of the triad, or of the chord of the seventh of the 3d degree (Sec. XI).

The second inversion of the diminished triad of the 7th degree **cannot** be succeeded by the harmony of the 6th degree (Sec. XI).

VII. II.—*By means of passing motions.*

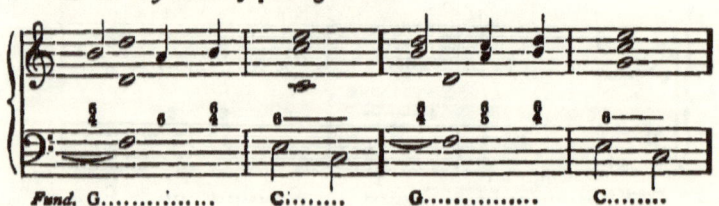

VII. IV.—*By means of passing motions.*

VII. V.—*By means of passing motions.*

THE HARMONIC SUCCESSIONS OF THE CHORD OF THE SEVENTH OF THE 7TH DEGREE.

VII. III.

VII. I.

VII. II.—*By means of passing motions.*

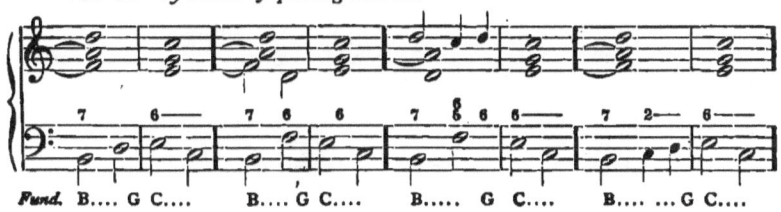

VII. IV.—*By means of passing motions.*

The mark ∧ implies that no other tones of the chord are required than those seen below it.

VII. V.—*By means of passing motions.*

VII. VI.—*By means of passing motions.*

THE HARMONIC SUCCESSIONS OF THE FIRST INVERSION OF THE CHORD OF THE SEVENTH OF THE 7TH DEGREE.

VII. III.

VII. I.

VII. II.—*By means of passing motions.*

VII. IV.—*By means of passing motions.*

VII. V.—*By means of passing motions.*

VII. VI.

The Harmonic Successions of the Second Inversion of the Chord of the Seventh of the 7th Degree.

VII. III.

VII. I.

VII. II.—*By means of passing motions.*

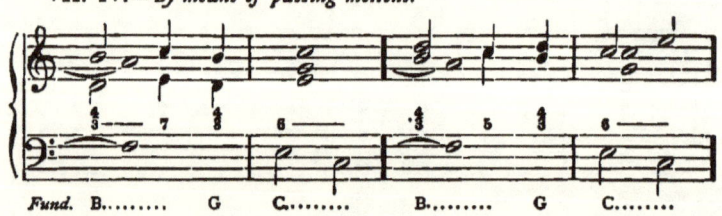

VII. IV.—*By means of passing motions.*

VII. V.—*By means of passing motions.*

THE HARMONIC SUCCESSIONS OF THE THIRD INVERSION OF THE CHORD OF THE SEVENTH OF THE 7TH DEGREE.

VII. III.

VII. II.—*By means of passing motions.*

VII. IV.—*By means of passing motions.*

VII. V.—*By means of passing motions.*

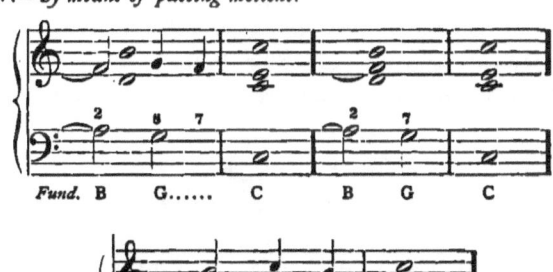

VII. VI.

PART II.

HARMONIC PROGRESSIONS IN THE DIATONIC MINOR SCALE.

INTRODUCTORY.

It being taken for granted that all the general rules and licenses explained in Part I are perfectly understood, new rules and licenses, appertaining to the *Minor Scale*, will now be discussed.

SECTION I.

The minor scale, which is characterized by a minor third and a minor sixth, exhibits a three-fold variety of progressions. The first and *most natural* progression of its component tones is, from the 1st to the 6th degree upward (from the 1st to the 2d degree, one step; from the 2d to the 3d, one diatonic half-step; from the 3d to the 4th, one step; from the 4th to the 5th, one step; and from the 5th to the 6th, one diatonic half-step), descending in the same order to the 1st, followed by the leading-tone of the scale, and concluding with the 1st degree. *E. g.*, in A minor:

In the second mode, in which an ascent is made from the 1st to the 8th degree, the 6th degree must be raised a chromatic half-step, in order to avoid the progression by an augmented second, in the step to the raised 7th degree (leading tone), which must be succeeded by the 8th degree. *E. g.*, in A minor:

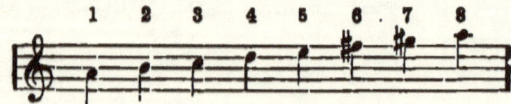

In the third mode, in which a descent is made from the 8th to the 1st degree, the 7th degree must be lowered a chromatic half-step, in order to effect a melodic step to the natural 6th degree, since all degrees must be natural. *E. g.*, in A minor :

The 1st, 2d, 3d, 4th and 5th degrees remain unchanged in each mode ; the only changeable degrees being the 6th and 7th, while the 8th degree remains unchanged, like the first.

The changes are thus easily explained :

1st.—The nature of the 6th degree after the 5th, depends upon the direct return to the 5th, or the ascent to the 7th degree. If the 6th degree is to be succeeded by the 5th, the former can be distant only a minor second, and must be natural. When the 6th degree is succeeded by the 7th, the former must be distant a major second, which is effected by raising it a chromatic half-step, in order to form a melodic step to the raised 7th degree (leading tone), which leads to the octave.

2d.—The nature of the 7th degree after the 8th, depends upon the direct return to the 8th, or the descent to the 6th degree. When the return to the 8th degree is intended, the 7th degree can be distant only a minor second, *i. e*, it must be raised. If the 7th degree is to be succeeded by the 6th, the former must be distant a major second, and therefore be natural, in order to form a melodic step to the natural 6th degree, which leads to the fifth.

Hence the following four modes in A minor, which will represent all other minor scales :

SECTION II.

The variable nature of the 6th and 7th degrees of the minor scale, gives rise to four *new intervals*, now to be discussed :

The *augmented second* arises from the simultaneous sounding of the *natural 6th* and *raised 7th* degrees :

The *diminished fourth* arises from the simultaneous sounding of the *raised 7th* and the 10*th* degrees :

The *augmented fifth* arises from the simultaneous sounding of the 3*d* and *raised 7th* degrees :

The *diminished seventh* arises from the simultaneous sounding of the *raised 7th* and *natural* 13*th* degrees :

The tones forming these four intervals must, in general, be introduced and progress according to the rules given in Section I.

SECTION III.

The character of the minor scale depends upon the perfect tuning of the minor triads of the 1st and 4th degrees, and of the major triad of the 5th degree.

A piano-forte tuned for the scale of C major, contains upon its 6th degree the perfect minor triad of A, which may be used for the tonic triad of A minor. In order to change the tuning from C major to A minor, it is necessary to tune the sub-dominant (D)—which in the major scale was too high by the ninth part of a step—so much lower, thereby restoring to the dubious minor third its right proportion. The minor triad of the 5th exists already upon the 3d degree in C major. Thus also the major triads of the 3d and natural 6th degrees, in A minor, exist upon the 1st and 4th degrees in C major.

The raised 6th and 7th degrees have now to be added to the other (natural) degrees as major thirds of the 4th and 5th degrees. In consequence of the lowering of the 4th degree (D) by the ninth part of a step, the fifth of the natural 7th degree will, in like proportion, approach its fundamental, and thereby exhibit the same dubious character in the minor scale, that the fifth of the 2d degree does in the major scale. The fifth of the 7th degree, accordingly, must be prepared, and resolved one degree downward.

Although the tuning of the piano-forte, according to the tempered system in vogue, does not exactly correspond with the theory above explained, still, the rules of the perfect system should be strictly adhered to.

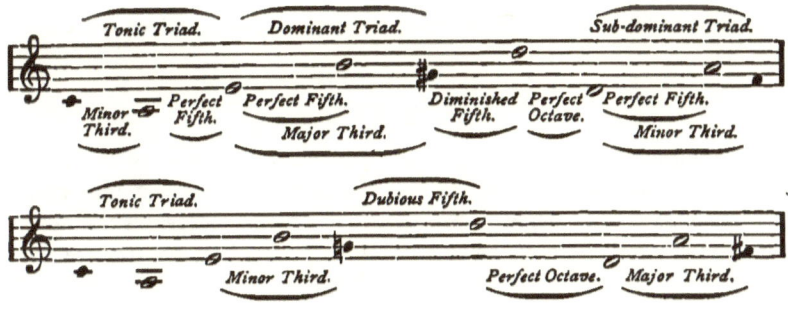

SECTION IV.

From the variable nature of the 6th and 7th degrees arises a greater number of triads in the minor than in the major scale.

The 1st degree is fundamental to a *minor* triad (*a*).

The 2d degree is fundamental to both a *diminished* and a *minor* triad (*b, c*).

The 3d degree is fundamental to both a *major* and an *augmented* triad (*d, e*).

The 4th degree is fundamental to both a *minor* and a *major* triad (*f, g*).

The 5th degree is fundamental to both a *minor* and a *major* triad (*h, i*).

The natural 6th degree is fundamental to a *major* triad (*j*).

The raised 6th degree is fundamental to a *diminished* triad (*k*).

The natural 7th degree is fundamental to a *major* triad (*l*).   Finally,

The raised 7th degree is fundamental to a *diminished* triad (*m*).

The minor triads of the 1st and 4th degrees, and the major triads of the 5th and natural 6th degrees, with their first inversions, may enter free and unprepared, seeing that they consist of tones characteristic of the minor scale.

The major triads of the 3d, 4th and natural 7th degrees, and the minor triads of the 2d and 5th degrees, cannot be considered as characteristic triads of the minor scale, because each of them contains one tone which is not strictly diatonic.

The diminished fifths of the 2d, raised 6th and 7th degrees, must be prepared, and resolved one degree downward. On the other hand, the augmented fifth of the 3d degree must be prepared, and resolved one degree upward.

SECTION V.

The upward tendency of the raised 6th and 7th degrees of the minor scale, precludes their standing as *sevenths*, in which character they would have to resolve one degree *downward*. Hence the 2d degree cannot be fundamental to a chord of the seventh with a perfect fifth, because the resolution of its seventh, *a*, and the upward tendency of its perfect fifth, *f♯*, would result in the duplication of the leading tone (raised 7th degree), *g♯*, which would involve parallel primes or octaves.

The 1st degree is fundamental to a chord of the seventh, consisting of a *minor* triad and a *minor seventh* (*a*).

The 2d degree is fundamental to a chord of the seventh, consisting of a *diminished triad* and a *minor seventh* (*b*).

The 3d degree is fundamental to a chord of the seventh, consisting of a *major triad* and a *major seventh* (*c*), and to another, consisting of an *augmented triad* and a *major seventh* (*d*).

The 4th degree is fundamental to a chord of the seventh, consisting of a *minor triad* and a *minor seventh* (*e*), and to another, consisting of a *major triad* and a *minor seventh* (*f*).

The 5th degree is fundamental to a chord of the seventh, consisting of a *minor triad* and a *minor seventh* (*g*), and to another, consisting of a *major triad* and a *minor seventh*, which latter is the *dominant chord of the seventh* (*h*).

The natural 6th degree is fundamental to a chord of the seventh, consisting of a *major triad* and a *major seventh* (*i*).

The raised 6th degree is fundamental to a chord of the seventh, consisting of a *diminished triad* and a *minor seventh* (*j*).

The natural 7th degree is fundamental to a chord of the seventh, consisting of a *major triad* and a *minor seventh* (*k*). Finally,

The raised 7th degree is fundamental to a chord of the seventh, consisting of a *diminished triad* and a *diminished seventh* (*l*).

The *dominant* chord of the seventh is the most harmonious. It may, alone of all chords of the seventh, enter free and unprepared.

SECTION VI.

The upward tendency of the raised 6th and 7th degrees forbids their standing as *ninths.* It also precludes their being *fundamental* to chords of the ninth, as their resolution would effect a duplication of the raised 6th and 7th degrees.

In the minor scale, the dominant chord of the seventh and ninth, and its inversions, are allowed to enter free and unprepared. The same license is extended to the diminished chord of the seventh of the raised 7th degree and its inversions, when standing as substitutes for the dominant chord of the seventh and ninth. The resolution of the ninth may be effected according to Sections XL, XLI and XLII of Part I of this treatise.

Here follow examples of the dominant chord of the seventh and ninth, and its inversions, with audible fundamental :

Examples of the diminished chord of the seventh of the raised 7th degree, and its inversions, as substitutes for the dominant chord of the seventh and ninth :

Delayed resolution of the dominant ninth (resolution with entrance of the new fundamental) :

Even the diminished triad of the 2d degree may stand as substitute for the dominant chord of the seventh and ninth, being, as such, succeeded by the first inversion of the tonic triad, *e. g.* :

The same examples more complete.

Fund. B E A   B E A   E   A   E   A

SECTION VII.

In all the following examples, the chord of the seventh of the raised 7th degree and all its inversions, may enter freely, when they stand as substitutes for the dominant chord of the seventh and ninth.

This case occurs :

1st.—After the tonic triad and its inversions.

2d.—After the dominant triad and its inversions. Even the diminished triad of the 2d degree may enter freely, if it stands as substitute for the dominant chord of the seventh and ninth.

(*ad* 1.)

Fund. A   E   A   E   A   E   A   E   A   E   A

(*ad* 2.)

Fund. A E A   E   E A....   E   E A......   E E...... A

Fund. A   E   E A E   E A....   E   E A E   E A.....

Fund. E   E A E   E A E A..........   E.......   A..........

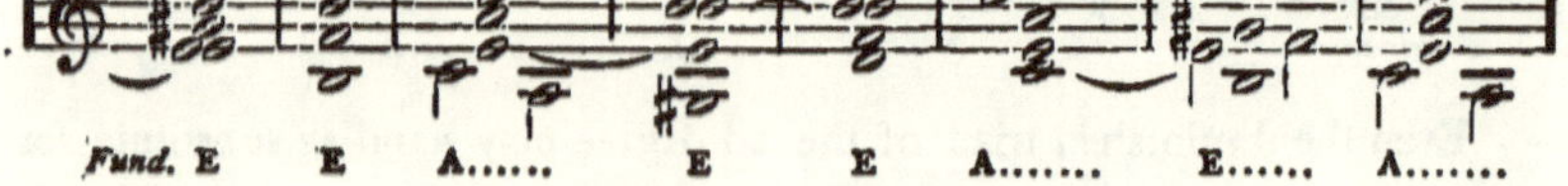

Fund. E   E A......   E   E A.......   E...... A.......

3d.—The seventh of the raised 7th degree may appear in another voice than that in which it is prepared ; but this occurs most appropriately after the diminished triad of the 2d, and after the minor triad of the 4th degree, and their inversions, *e. g.* :

Fund. A   D   B   E...........   Ā   A   D   B   E........... . Ā

Fund. A   F   B   E...........   A   A   D B E.........   A

Fund. A   D B E...........   A   A   D   G♯ E A   A   D B E   A
or : A   D B   E   A

SECTION VIII.

During the continuance of the same fundamental, the component tones of the chord may exchange their positions, as explained in Sections XVII and XVIII of Part I. The said exchanges may also take place in any chord containing the natural or raised 6th or 7th degrees, and be linked together by means of passing tones, *e. g.* :

Exchange.   *With passing tones.*

Fund. D........   D...... .   D..........   D..........

Exchange.   *With passing tones.*

Fund. D........   D........   D..........   D..........

Exchange.   *With passing tones.*

Exchanges during the continuance of the chord of the seventh of the natural 6th degree.

The same with passing tones.

Exchanges during the continuance of the chord of the seventh of the natural 7th degree.

The same with passing tones.

The contradiction which seems to exist between the the preceding examples and the rules laid down in Section I, regarding the upward tendency of the natural and raised 6th and 7th degrees, is explained by the fact, that the progressions in these examples are effected, not by *essential harmonic tones*, but by the insertion of *passing tones*, as explained in Section **XIX** of Part I.

SECTION IX.

In the minor, as well as in the major scale, each of its tones may ascend or descend one degree, to return again. The following examples therefore are perfectly legitimate.

It is evident that in the above examples the descent of the raised 6th and 7th, and the ascent of the natural 6th and 7th degrees, are effected not by *essential* or *harmonic*, but by *passing* tones.

SECTION X.

Passing motions (returning and melodic connections), may also occur with the step of the octave to the passing seventh, *e. g.:*

The progression exemplified below, has not yet been noticed. Whenever it occurs, an exchange takes place between the seventh and fifth, during the continuance of the same fundamental, which, however, can be applied without reserve, *only with* the dominant chord of the seventh, *e. g.:*

In order to make an application of this progression to the chord of the seventh of other degrees, we now permit one of the voices to skip from the fifth to the octave, instead of from the fifth to the seventh, after which, as a matter of course, the passing seventh may follow. We then permit the other voice to descend gradually from the seventh to the sixth and fifth, instead of skipping from the seventh to the fifth. In this way the seventh, by means of the *passing sixth* (which is no part of the fundamental harmony), receives what is termed the *passing* resolution, to distinguish it from the *actual* resolution, *e. g.*

This progression may be repeated with each fundamental descent by a fifth, or may alternate with a triad harmony. When, however, it occurs with the chord of the seventh of the 2d degree, it must be repeated on the dominant.

This progression cannot be effected with the chord of the seventh of the raised 6th and 7th degrees, because these cannot be doubled ; nor with the chord of the seventh of the 3d degree with augmented fifth, because the augmented fifth would have to skip, contrary to the rule.

SECTION XI.

Two regular progressions from the same fundamental are possible ; the descent by a fifth (ascent by a fourth), or by a third.

The ascent of the fundamental by a fifth or third is dependent upon the perfection or independence of both chords, the first chord requiring no resolution, and the second, no preparation. This leaves but the following perfect progressions :

(*a*). The ascent by a fifth :

From the tonic triad to either of the triads of the 5th degree.

From the sub-dominant triad, to the tonic triad.

From the triad of the natural 6th to the major triad of the 3d degree.

(*b*). The ascent by a third :

From the tonic triad to the major triad of the 3d degree.

From the subdominant triad to the triad of the natural 6th degree.

From the triad of the natural 6th degree to the tonic triad.

From the major triad of the 3d to the minor triad of the 5th degree.

In the remaining progressions of the fundamentals ascending by a third, the second triad must be treated as substitute for a chord of the seventh of the first fundamental.

The seeming ascent of the fundamental by a fifth from the other degrees, as referred to above, is explained by the fact, that the second triad is regarded as an incomplete chord of the seventh and ninth of the first fundamental.

SECTION XII.

The ascending tendency of the raised 6th and 7th degrees of the minor scale, considerably limits their standing as fundamentals, owing to their inability to descend by a fifth or third, which progressions have been already pointed out as the only regular ones of the fundamental. These degrees may, nevertheless, stand as fundamentals, if the rules set down in Sections I, V and VI are adhered to, the only licenses granted being those explained in Sections VIII and IX.

SECTION XIII.

The formation of the *closing cadence* in the minor scale supposes such a grouping of the degrees of the scale, as shall make the characteristic tones appear most prominent.   It may be effected, either by the succession of the minor triad of the 4th degree, the dominant triad (or dominant chord of the seventh) and the triad of the 1st degree (*a*) ; or by that of the diminished triad (or its corresponding chord of the seventh) of the 2d degree, the dominant triad (or the chord of the seventh *)*, and the triad of the 1st degree (*b*).

Other closing cadences may be effected by the succession of the major triads of the 4th and 5th degrees, and the minor triad of the 1st degree (*a*), or, by the minor triad of the 2d, the major triad (or the chord of the seventh) of the 5th, and minor triad of the 1st degrees (*b*) ; but these are cadences not so satisfactory as the former.

SECTION XIV.

1st.—In the succession of the triads of the 1st, 5th and 1st degrees, the triad of the 5th degree must contain a *major third*, which makes it the true dominant triad, *e. g.:*

2d.—In the succession of the triads of the 1st, 4th and 1st degrees, the triad of the 4th degree must contain a *minor third*, which makes it the true subdominant triad, *e. g.:*

These examples illustrate the chief characteristic progressions in the minor scale, and exhibit the close relation of the triads of the dominant and subdominant to that of the tonic.

3d.—The succession of the minor triads of the 1st and 5th degrees, cannot again be followed by that of the 1st degree, since the minor third, *g*, of the fifth degree, *e*, cannot ascend; but it may remain as seventh of the 1st degree, to be followed by the regular succession of the fundamentals, until a close is reached. *E. g.:*

In this example, the soprano shows the descent in the minor scale from the 8th to the 5th degrees.

4th.—The succession of the minor triad of the 1st and the major triad of the 4th degree, cannot be again followed by the minor triad of the 1st degree, because the major third, *f♯*, of the 4th degree, *d*, cannot descend; but it may remain as perfect fifth of the 2d degree, to ascend to the major third of the 5th, and resolve into the octave of the 1st degree. *E. g.:*

5th.—The triad of the natural 6th degree follows naturally after that of the 1st, and is succeeded by the *diminished* triad of the 2d degree, *etc.*

6th.—The triad of the raised 6th degree is also most naturally preceded by that of the first, and succeeded by the *minor* triad of the 2d degree, *etc.*

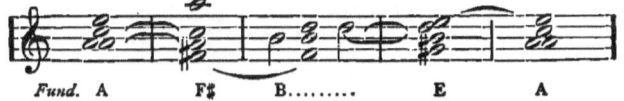

7th.—The major triad of the 3d degree may also be preceded by the triad of the 1st, and be succeeded by that of the natural 6th degree, *etc.*

8th.—The triad of the 1st cannot be immediately succeeded by the augmented triad of the 3d degree, as the latter should be preceded by the major triad of the 5th, and followed by that of the natural 6th degree, *etc.*

SECTION XV.

Having explained the harmonic successions to the triad of the 1st degree, we shall now discuss the conditions of the entrance of and successions to the remaining triads, as these have not the independence of the former.

1st.—The diminished triad of the 2d degree must be preceded by the triad of the natural 6th, or by the minor triad of the 4th degree, and be succeeded by the dominant harmony.

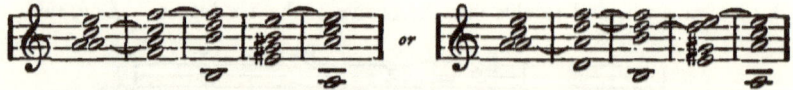

2d.—The minor triad of the 2d degree enters most naturally after the major triad of the 4th, or the 1st inversion of the harmony of the raised 6th degree. It is succeeded by the dominant harmony. *E. g.:*

3d.—The major triad of the 3d degree may be preceded by the triad of the 1st and by that of the 5th degree, and also by the harmony of the natural 7th degree. It is best succeeded by the triad of the natural 6th degree.

4th.—That the augmented triad of the 3d degree is best preceded by the dominant harmony, has been shown (Sect. XIV, 8). It may be succeeded by the harmony of the raised, as well as by that of the natural 6th degree.

Fund. A   E   C   F♯   B   E   A

Fund. A   E   C   F♯ . B   E   A

But this same triad may be preceded also by the second or first inversion of the harmony of the raised 7th degree, and be succeeded by the triad of the 1st degree, by means of which, however, no close is yet reached, since the latter can be obtained only by regular fundamental progressions. *E. g.:*

Fund. A   D   G♯   C   A.......   F   B   E   A

Fund. A   D   G♯   C   A   D   B   E   A

5th.—That the minor triad of the 4th degree can be preceded by that of the 1st degree, has been shown; but it may also be preceded by the triad of the natural 6th degree. It is succeeded by the diminished triad of the 2d degree, etc., whenever a close is intended: if not, it may be followed by the triad of the 1st degree, *e. g.:*

6th.—The major triad of the 4th degree can, strictly speaking, be preceded only by the triad of the 1st degree. In Section XIV, 4, it was succeeded by the minor triad of the 2d degree; though it may also be followed by the first inversion of the triad of the raised 7th degree, after which a close may be reached by the successions of the dominant harmony and of the triad of the 1st degree, *e. g.:*

Fund. A   D   G♯   E   A

7th.—That the major triad of the 5th degree may be preceded by the triad of the 1st, or by the diminished or minor triad of the 2d degree, we have seen repeatedly. It has also been shown that this triad of the 5th degree may be succeeded by that of the 1st, or by the augmented triad of the 3d degree.

8th.—That the minor triad of the 5th degree may be preceded by that of the 1st degree, has been exemplified. But it may also be preceded by the major triad of the 3d, or by that of the natural 7th degree, although without exhibiting any characteristic of the minor scale. It cannot follow after the diminished triad of the 2d degree, because the nature of the minor scale demands the characteristic succession of the major triad of the 5th degree. The minor triad of the 5th degree, may be succeeded ·by the major triad of the 3d degree.

9th.—That the triad of the natural 6th degree may be preceded by the triad of the 1st, or the major triad of the 3d degree, we have already seen ; yet it may also follow after the minor triad of the 4th degree. This triad of the 6th degree may be succeeded by the diminished triad of the 2d, or by the minor triad of the 4th degree.

Moreover, this triad may be followed by that of the 1st degree, but without forming a close, as this must be reached in the usual manner, *e. g.* :

10th.—The triad of the raised 6th degree is preceded most generally by that of the 1st, or by the augmented triad of the 3d degree, as in both cases the diminished fifth of the raised 6th degree is prepared. This diminished fifth will be resolved by the succession of the minor triad of the 2d degree, or one of its inversions, *e. g.* :

11th.—The triad of the natural 7th degree needs a preparation on account of its fifth, that is, it must be preceded by the minor triad of the 4th degree. The resolution of this fifth is obtained by the succession of the major triad of the 3d degree, etc. *E. g.* :

12th.—The triad of the raised 7th degree must be preceded by the minor or major triad of the 4th, or by one of the inversions of the minor triad of the 2d degree. The diminished fifth of the raised 7th degree is resolved by the succession of an inversion of the augmented triad of the 3d degree. *E. g.:*

SECTION XVI.

THE PREPARATION OF THE CHORDS OF THE SEVENTH.

1st.—The chord of the seventh of the 5th degree, with major third, may enter freely, though it may be prepared by the triad or chord of the seventh of the 2d degree with diminished fifth; by the minor triad of the 2d, or by the diminished triad of the raised 7th degree. *E. g.:*

If it is preceded by the minor triad of the 4th degree, the latter must be treated as substitute for the chord of the seventh of the 2d degree, without fundamental, as is seen in the following examples :

More correctly :

If it is preceded by the major triad of the 4th degree, the latter must occur without fifth, since this seeming triad of the 4th degree stands but as substitute for the chord of the seventh of the 2d degree, as is seen in the following examples :

More correctly :

2d.—The chord of the seventh of the 5th degree, with a *minor* third, is the most unusual. It is best introduced by means of passing motion after the minor triad of the same degree, and should be succeeded by the chord of the seventh of the 1st degree, which may be followed by the minor triad of the 4th degree, etc., *e. g. :*

3d.—The chord of the seventh of the 2d degree always contains a diminished fifth, and is prepared by the minor triad of the 4th, or by the triad of the natural 6th degree. It should be succeeded by the major triad, or the corresponding chord of the seventh, of the 5th degree, etc., *e. g. :*

If this chord of the seventh is preceded by the tonic triad, the latter stands as substitute for the chord of the seventh of the natural 6th degree, without fundamental, *e. g. :*

More correctly :

4th.—The chord of the seventh of the natural 6th degree may be prepared by means of the tonic triad, or the major triad of the 3d degree. It resolves most naturally into the diminished triad, or the corresponding chord of the seventh, of the 2d degree, etc., *e. g.* :

If this chord of the seventh is preceded by the minor triad of the 5th degree, the latter must be treated as substitute for the chord of the seventh of the 3d degree, with perfect fifth, but without fundamental, as is seen in the following example :

More correctly :

If this chord of the seventh is preceded by the major triad of the 5th degree, the latter stands but as substitute for the chord of the seventh of the 3d degree, with an augmented fifth, *e. g.* :

5th.—The chord of the seventh of the raised 6th degree, is best preceded by the tonic triad, or the augmented triad of the 3d degree, to resolve into the 2d inversion of the minor triad of the 2d degree, *e. g.* :

Fund. A   F♯   B   E   A

Fund. A   E   C   F♯   B   E   A

Whenever this chord of the seventh is preceded by the major triad of the 5th degree, it stands as substitute for the chord of the seventh of the 3d degree, with an augmented fifth, *e. g.*:

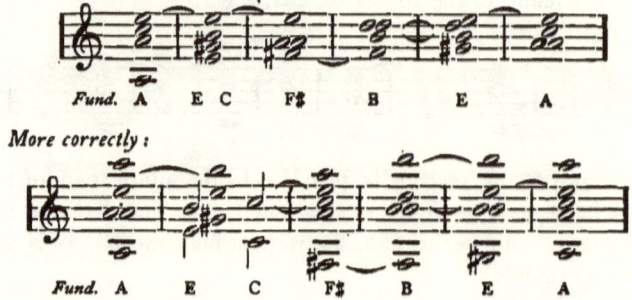

More correctly:

6th.—The chord of the seventh of the 3d degree, with a perfect fifth, may be preceded by the minor triad of the 5th, or the triad of the natural 7th degree. This chord of the seventh may be succeeded by the triad, or the chord of the seventh, of the natural 6th degree, etc., *e. g.*:

If this chord of the seventh occurs without fifth, after the diminished triad of the 2d degree, this triad stands as a substitute for the chord of the seventh of the natural, or raised 7th degree, *e. g.*:

More correctly:

Or:

7th.—The chord of the seventh of the 3d degree, with an augmented fifth, is best preceded by the major triad of the 5th, or by the second inversion of the triad, or chord of the seventh, of the raised 7th degree, to resolve into the triad, or chord of the seventh, of the natural or raised 6th degree, or rather into its second inversion, etc., *e. g.*:

8th.—The chord of the seventh of the natural 7th degree, may be preceded by the minor triad, or the corresponding chord of the seventh, of the 4th degree, or, seemingly by the diminished triad of the 2d degree, to resolve into the major triad, or the corresponding chord of the seventh, of the 3d degree, etc, *e. g.*:

9th.—The chord of the seventh of the raised 7th degree, may also be preceded by the minor triad, or the corresponding chord of the seventh, of the 4th degree, to resolve into the second inversion of the augmented triad, or corresponding chord of the seventh, of the 3d degree, etc, *e. g.*:

10th.—The chord of the seventh of the 4th degree, with minor third, may be preceded by the triad, or chord of the seventh, of the 1st degree, or by the triad of the natural 6th degree, to resolve only into the chord of the seventh of the natural, or raised 7th degree, or its second inversion, etc, *e. g.*:

If this chord of the seventh occurs without fifth, after the major triad of the 3d degree, it stands as substitute for the chord of the seventh of the 1st degree, *e. g.*:

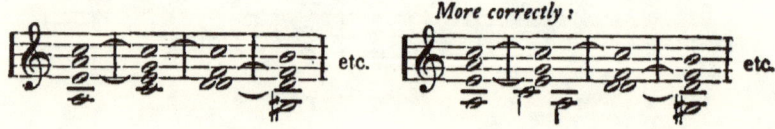

11th.—The chord of the seventh of the 4th degree, with major third, may be preceded by the triad of the 1st, or the first inversion of the triad of the raised 6th degree, to resolve into the second inversion of the triad of the raised 7th degree, *e. g.* :

12th.—The chord of the seventh of the 1st degree may be preceded by the minor triad, or by the corresponding chord of the seventh of the 5th, or the major triad of the 3d degree, to resolve into the minor triad, or corresponding chord of the seventh, of the 4th degree, *e. g.* :

etc.

SECTION XVII.

Whenever, in the progression from the *major triad of the 4th* to the *chord of the seventh of the 5th degree* with a *major third*, the former occurs with its fifth, it stands as substitute for the chord of the seventh of the 2d degree with perfect fifth, which was rejected. Considering that this fifth of the 2d degree must ascend to the leading tone, whither the seventh also tends, and that a duplication of the leading tone is forbidden, it remains only that the seventh should ascend, which, in this case, is quite proper, inasmuch as its fundamental is inaudible. This progression of the ascending seventh is allowable only when the third occurs above it, as otherwise consecutive fifths would arise. Hence, the major triad of the 4th degree with its fifth, should be succeeded, not by the dominant chord of the seventh itself, but by its third inversion, the chord of the second. The case is the same, if the first inversion of the major triad of the 4th degree is succeeded by the first inversion of the dominant chord of the seventh. *E. g.:*

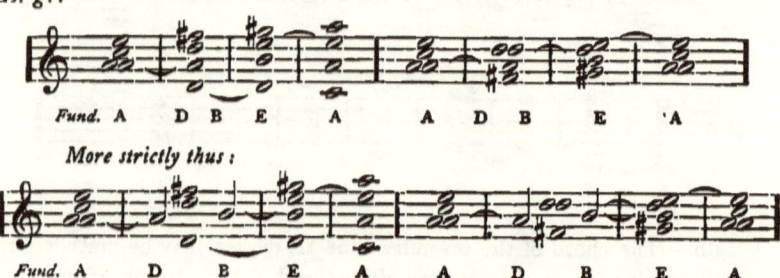

Fund. A   D B E   A   A   D B   E   ·A

More strictly thus:

Fund. A   D   B   E   A   A   D   B   E   A

The directions just given for the above progressions, may also be applied to the following analogous cases : (*a*) when the harmony of the chord of the seventh of the *natural 7th degree* is preceded by the triad of the *natural 6th degree ;* (*b*) when the harmony of the chord of the seventh of the *raised 7th degree* is preceded by the triad of the *natural 6th degree ;* and (*c*) when the harmony of the chord of the seventh of the *1st degree* is preceded by the triad of the *natural 7th degree.*

(*a*)

Fund. A   F D G   C   F   B   E   A

Fund. A   F D G   C   F   B   E.   A

(*b*)

Fund. A   F D G♯   C   F   B   E   A

Fund. A   F D G♯   C   F♯   B   E   A

(c)

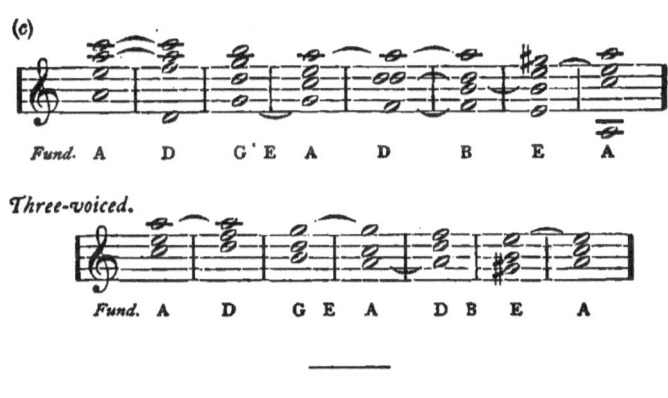

Fund. A   D   G·E   A   D   B   E   A

Three-voiced.

Fund. A   D   G E   A   D B   E   A

SECTION XVIII.

The directions given in Section XXXIII, Part I, regarding the ascent of the fundamental by degrees, apply equally to the minor scale, and will be illustrated by some examples.

1st.—Whenever the tonic triad is followed by the diminished triad of the 2d degree, the former stands as substitute for the chord of the seventh of the natural 6th degree.

The free entrance of the diminished fifth is allowable, when the other voices progress regularly ; still, it is better to substitute for the triad of the 2d degree its first inversion, thereby enabling the diminished fifth to appear as third of the bass, with a more satisfactory result. *E. g.:*

Or rather :

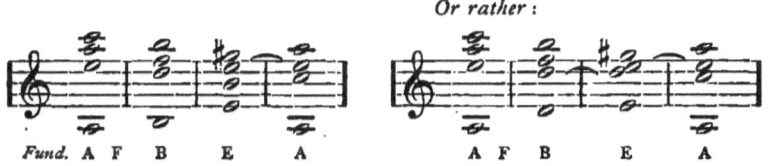

Fund. A F   B   E   A   A F   B   E   A

Whenever the tonic triad is succeeded by the minor triad of the 2d degree, the former stands only as substitute for the chord of the seventh of the raised 6th degree. *E. g.:*

More correctly :

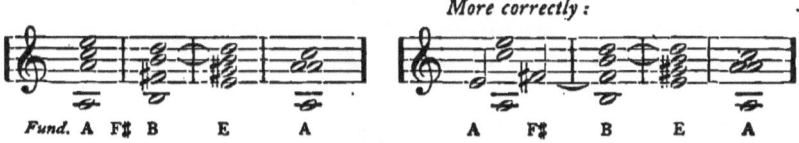

Fund. A F♯ B   E   A   A   F♯   B   E   A

2d.—If the diminished triad of the 2d degree is succeeded by the major triad of the 3d degree (which is contrary to the character of the minor scale), the former must be treated as substitute for the chord of the seventh of the natural 7th degree. *E. g.*:

More correctly :

3d.—When the diminished triad of the 2d is followed by the augmented triad of the third degree, (which succession is extremely unharmonious, owing to the free entrance of the augmented fifth,) the former must be treated as substitute for the chord of the seventh of the raised 7th degree, if the latter occurs independent. *E. g.*:

More correctly :

4th.—If the major triad of the 3d is followed by the minor triad of the 4th degree, the former stands as substitute for the chord of the seventh of 1st degree. *E. g*:

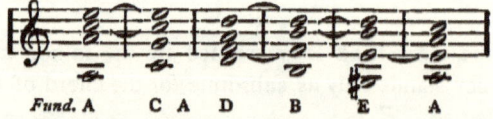

5th.—When the minor triad of the 4th is followed by the major triad of the 5th degree, the former stands as substitute for the chord of the seventh, of the 2d degree, with diminished fifth. *E. g.*:

More correctly :

N. B.—Since the succession of the minor triad of the 4th and the major triad of the 5th degree, can be effected only by means of the real or seeming chord of the seventh of the 2d degree, it is evident that the former cannot be followed by the minor triad of the 5th degree.

6th.—Whenever the minor triad of the 5th is succeeded by the triad of the natural 6th degree, the former stands as substitute for the chord of the seventh of the 3d degree, with a perfect fifth. *E. g.:*

More correctly:

7th.—If the major triad of the 5th is succeeded by the triad of the natural 6th degree, the former stands as substitute for the chord of the seventh of the 3d degree, with augmented fifth. *E. g.:*

8th.—If the triad of the raised 6th is to be succeeded by the triad of the raised 7th degree (a progression which may be allowed for the sake of practice, although it is far from being euphonious, for the reason that the diminished fifth of the raised 7th degree enters free), it follows, that the former stands as substitute for the first inversion of the chord of the seventh, of the 4th degree, with major third. *E. g.:*

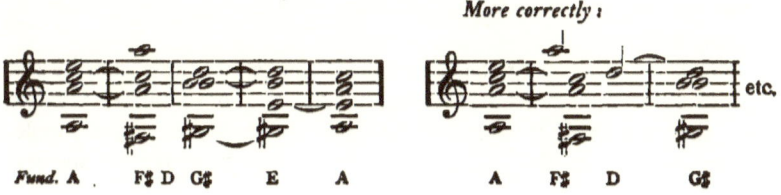

9th.—Whenever the triad of the raised 7th is succeeded by that of the 1st degree, the former must be considered as substitute for the first inversion of the chord of the seventh of the 5th degree, with a major third. *E. g.:*

More correctly:

Fund. A   D   G♯ E A   A   D   G♯   E   A

SECTION XIX.

The formation of suspensions in the minor scale must be effected in the same manner as in the major scale, with this modification however, that the raised 6th and 7th degrees cannot be used as suspensions *from above*, while the natural 6th and 7th degrees cannot serve as suspensions *from below*.

The *ascending seventh* occurs upon the 1st, 3d and natural 6th degrees.

SUPPLEMENTARY REMARKS.

Since the chords appertaining to the minor scale contain a greater number of dissonances, and other tones, viz : the raised 6th and the natural 7th degrees, which latter, strictly speaking, are foreign to the nature of the minor scale, care must be taken during the study of the exercises relating to them, that their entrances and progressions be effected in exact conformity with the rules laid down. The *descent* of the fundamental by a fifth (ascent by a fourth), or by a third, requires no additional explanation, but the *ascent* of the fundamental by a fifth (descent by a fourth), or by a third, involving progressions other than those which in Section XI were pronounced unexceptionable, must be effected in accordance with the directions given in Sections XXX, XXXI, XXXII, XXXVII, and XLII—XLIV of Part I of this treatise, and be perfected by means of exchanges, passing motions, and suspensions.

Practice in connecting the harmonies of the minor scale, may be best obtained by writing exercises, following the order laid down in the subjoined table, and transposing them into the different minor scales. The supplementary remarks at the end of Part I will here be found of practical application.

.TABLE.

$\overset{\sharp}{V}$: 1, 6, ♭, $\overset{\cancel{5}}{3}$, 4, $\overset{\sharp}{4}$, ♭7, 2, $\overset{\cancel{5}}{2}$.

V : 1, 3, 6, 4, 7, 2.

IV : 7, ♭7, 2, 6, $\overset{\sharp}{5}$, 5, 3, 1.

$\overset{\sharp}{IV}$: ♭7, $\overset{\cancel{5}}{2}$, ♭6, $\overset{\cancel{5}}{3}$, 1, $\overset{\sharp}{5}$.

II : $\overset{\sharp}{5}$, 5, 1, 3, 4, 7, ♭7, 6.

$\overset{\cancel{5}}{II}$: 5, $\overset{\sharp}{4}$, $\overset{\sharp}{3}$, $\overset{\cancel{5}}{1}$, ♭7, ♭6.

VI : 2, 4, 1, 3, $\overset{\cancel{5}}{3}$, 5, 7, ♭7.

$\sharp$VI : $\overset{\cancel{5}}{2}$, ♭7, $\overset{\sharp}{5}$, $\overset{\sharp}{4}$, 1, $\overset{\cancel{5}}{3}$.

III : 6, 1, 5, 7, 4, 2.

$\overset{\cancel{5}}{III}$: $\overset{\cancel{5}}{2}$, 2, 6, ♭, 1, 4, $\overset{\sharp}{4}$, ♭7, $\overset{\sharp}{5}$.

VII : 3, 5, 1, 6, 2, 4.

$\sharp$VII : 3, 6, $\overset{\cancel{5}}{♭}$, $\overset{\sharp}{5}$, 1, 2, $\overset{\cancel{5}}{2}$, 4, $\overset{\sharp}{4}$.

I : 4, $\overset{\sharp}{4}$, $\overset{\sharp}{5}$, 5, 6, ♭, 3, $\overset{\cancel{5}}{3}$, 2, $\overset{\cancel{5}}{2}$, 7, ♭7.

By way of explanation of the above table, we would remark that the Roman numbers indicate the harmony of that degree which is considered as a starting-point. The student should set himself the problem of joining to this harmony, as far as is practicable, the harmonies of the respective degrees indicated by Arabic numbers. The sharps placed above the ciphers indicate that the harmony of the respective degrees must contain a major third; the figure five with a dash ($\cancel{5}$) signifies, with the 2d degree, the harmony with the perfect—, and with the 3d degree, the harmony with the augmented fifth. The numbers ♭ and ♭7, with a dash, indicate raised degrees, as do also the Roman numbers preceded by a sharp ($\sharp$VI and $\sharp$VII). In all other cases, the harmony of the respective degrees must be composed of natural tones.

PART III.

_____

DIATONIC MODULATION.

_____

INTRODUCTORY.

MODULATION may be defined, a *change of tonic, or key, i. e.*, a transferring of the character of *tonic* to a tone which did not possess it before.

Diatonic modulation from one scale or key into another, is effected only by means of their diatonic tones, in so far, that is, as the same chord which stands in the first scale upon the 1st degree, is found on another degree in the second.

Now, in order to show how we may modulate in all cases by means of diatonic progression, it is necessary to make use of every scale from C♭ to C♯ major, and from A♭ to A♯ minor. Those who hold that it is one and the same thing whether they modulate into the scales of F♯ or G♭ major, into B or C♭ major, into C♯ or D♭ major; or into those of A♯ or B♭ minor, G♯ or A♭ minor, and D♯ or E♭ minor, may, by means of this treatise, be easily convinced of the contrary. If the modulations by diatonic means are found to be more extensive, and to require more chords, they have, on the other hand, the advantage of being more positive and precise, than the chromatic and enharmonic modulations.

_____

SECTION I.

A triad is readily recognized as a tonic triad, if it is preceded by its dominant harmony and its subdominant triad, *e. g.*:

$$\text{I IV I V I, or: I IV I } \overset{7}{\text{V}} \text{ I.}$$

It has been seen, that the succession of the subdominant triad and dominant harmony should be connected by the actual or tacit harmony of the 2d degree, which would give the following fundamental progressions :

$$\text{I IV II V I, or: I IV II } \overset{7}{\text{V}} \text{ I, or: I IV } \overset{7}{\text{II}} \overset{7}{\text{V}} \text{ I.}$$

But since the chord of the seventh of the 2d degree contains all the component parts of the triad of the 4th degree, the latter may be omitted at discretion, whenever the former is preceded by the triad or chord of the seventh of the 6th degree, *e. g.* :

I VI II^7 V I, or: I VI II $\overset{7}{V}$ I, or: I VI II $\overset{7}{V}$ I.

When this succession is to be extended, the harmony of the 6th may be preceded by that of the 3d degree, *e. g.* :

I III VI II^7 V I, or: I III $\overset{7}{VI}$ II^7 $\overset{7}{V}$ I, or: I III $\overset{7}{VI}$ II^7 $\overset{7}{V}$ I.

If the subdominant triad is succeeded by the harmony of the 7th degree, the harmonic passage will be still more extended, if the latter is followed by the harmony of the 3d degree, etc., *e. g.* :

I IV VII III VI II V I, or: I IV $\overset{7}{VII}$ III^7 $\overset{7}{VI}$ II^7 $\overset{7}{V}$ I.

All these progressions may be effected by means of primary chords, or their inversions.

SECTION II.

A. The major triads occur, in the major scale, upon the 1st, 4th and 5th degrees, and in the minor scale upon the 3d, 4th and 5th and the natural 6th and 7th degrees. Hence, each of the above named degrees may be fundamental to the same major triad. *E. g.* : The major triad of C occurs upon the 1st degree of the scale of C major, upon the 4th degree of G major, and upon the 5th degree of F major ; it occurs also upon the 3d degree of A minor, upon the 4th degree of G minor, upon the 5th degree of F minor, upon the natural 6th degree of E minor, and upon the natural 7th degree of D minor.

B. The minor triads occur : in the major scale upon the 2d, 3d and 6th, and in the minor scale upon the 1st, 2d, 4th and 5th degrees. Hence, each of the above named degrees may be fundamental to the same minor triad. *E. g.* : The minor triad of A occurs upon the 2d degree of G major, upon the 3d degree of F major, and upon the 6th degree of C major, and also upon the 1st degree of A minor, upon the 2d degree of G minor, upon the 4th degree of E minor, and upon the 5th degree of D minor.

Only major or minor triads can become tonic triads.

The following Section contains the modulations from C major into its relative scales, and also the returns of those modulations into their original scale.   The examples will be the better understood by means of the added fundamentals, and the Roman ciphers, which mark the degrees in each particular modulation.

SECTION III.

From C major into G major:

        C   A   D   G

Degrees in G major: IV   II   V   I

From G major into C major:

        G C   F D G C

Degrees in C major: V I   IV II V I

From C major into F major:

        G   F   B♭ G C   F

Degrees in F major: V I   IV. II V I

From F major into C major:

        F   D   G   C

Degrees in C major: IV II V I

From C major into A minor:

        C   F   B   E   A

Degrees in A minor: III VI II V I

From A minor into C major:

        A   D   G   C

Degrees in C major: VI II V I

From C major into E minor:

        C   F♯   B   E

Degrees in E minor: VI II V I

From E minor into C major:

        E   A   D   G   C

Degrees in C major: III VI II V I

From C major into D minor:

	C	F	Bb	E	A	D
Degrees in D minor:	VII	III	VI	II	V	I

From D minor into C major :

	D	G	C
Degrees in C major :	II	V	I

From C major into G minor :

	C	A	D	G
Degrees in G minor :	IV ·	II	V	I

In order to effect a return of the modulation from G minor into C major, a mediation is necessary, because the minor triad of G is not contained in the scale of C major. This mediation, or intermediate scale, may be that of F major or D minor, both of which contain the minor triad of G. After having effected the modulation into F major, we treat its tonic triad as standing upon the 4th degree of C major. If a modulation is made into D minor, its tonic triad is treated as standing upon the 2d degree of C major, from which degree, as well as from the 4th, the major triad of C is easily reached. *E. g.:*

From G minor into F major :

	G	C	F
Degrees in F major :	II	V	I

From F major into C major :

	F	D	G	C
Degrees in C major :	IV	II	V	I

From G minor into D minor :

	G	E	A	D
Degrees in D minor :	IV	II	V	I

From D minor into C major :

	D	G	C
Degrees in C major :	II	V	I

From C major into F minor :

	C	F	Bb	G	C	F
Degrees in F minor :	V	I	IV	II	V	I

The modulation from F minor back into C major, must again be effected by means of an intermediate scale, because the minor triad of F is not contained in the scale of C major. To do this, we treat the minor triad of F as standing upon the 4th degree of C minor, which is then succeeded, first, by the harmony of the 2d degree, and next, by the dominant harmony of that scale. The homogeneous nature of the dominant harmony in the major and minor scales, offers then the best opportunity to resolve into the major rather than into the minor scale.

From F minor into C minor, resolving into C major:

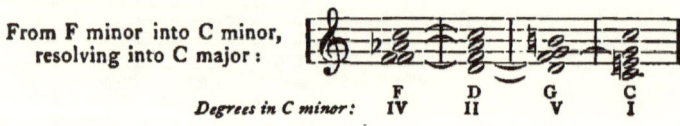

Degrees in C minor:

F	D	G	C
IV	II	V	I

SECTION IV.

Modulations from A minor into its relative scales, with returning modulations into A minor.

From A minor into G major:

Degrees in G major:

A	D	G
II	V	I

From G major into A minor:

Degrees in A minor:

G	C	F	B	E	A
VII	III	VI	II	V	I

From A minor into F major:

Degrees in F major:

A	D	G	C	F
III	VI	II	V	I

From F major into A minor:

Degrees in A minor:

F	B	E	A
VI	II	V	I

From A minor into C major:

Degrees in C major:

A	D	G	C
VI	II	V	I

From C major into A minor:

Degrees in A minor:

C	F	B	E	A
III	VI	II	V	I

From A minor into E minor:

	A	F♯	B	E
Degrees in E minor :	IV	II	V	I

From E minor into A minor:

	E	C	F	B	E	A
Degrees in A minor :	V	III	VI	II	V	I

From A minor into D minor :

	A	F	B♭	E	A	D
Degrees in D minor :	V	III	VI	II	V	I

From D minor into A minor :

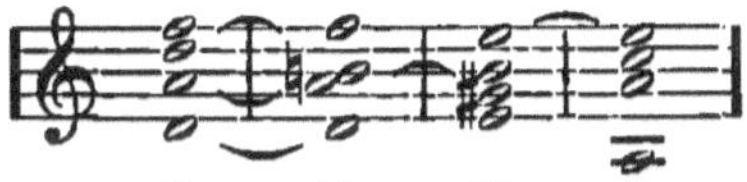

	D	B	E	A
Degrees in A minor :	IV	II	V	I

From A minor into G minor :

	A	D	G
Degrees in G minor :	II	V	I

The modulation from G minor back into A minor, must be effected by means of an intermediate scale, as the minor triad of G is not contained in the scale of A minor. This intermediate scale may be that of D minor or of F major. From the modulation into F major we obtain the triad of the natural 6th degree, and from that into D minor, the minor triad of the 4th degree of A minor, from either of which degrees a close may be reached by the regular fundamental progressions. *E. g.* :

From G minor into F major :

	G	C	F
Degrees in F major :	II	V	I

From F major into A minor :

	F	B	E	A
Degrees in A minor :	VI	II	V	I

From G minor into D minor :

G   E   A   D

Degrees in D minor :   IV   II   V   I

From D minor into A minor :

D   B   E   A

Degrees in A minor :   IV   II   V   I

SECTION V.

The following table will materially assist us in obtaining a general summary of the scales more closely or more distantly related to C major, which stands in the centre. From its right, extend the scales as they increase in the number of sharps, and from its left, as they increase in flats. Immediately below the scale of C major stands that of A minor, and similarly, under every other major scale, stands that minor scale with which it has a common signature. The major scales are marked by capitals, and the minor scales by small letters.

C♭, G♭, D♭, A♭, E♭, B♭, F, **C**, G, D, A, E, B, F♯, C♯.

a♭ e♭, b♭, f, c, g, d, **a**, e, b, f♯, c♯, g♯, d♯, a♯.

Now, just as the scale of C major is akin to the scales of G and F major, which stand nearest to it on both sides, and since it is also related to those of A minor, E minor, and D minor, which stand right below the above named major scales, and, moreover, to the three minor scales of G, C, and F, standing still more towards the left, it follows that every major scale bears a relation to both major scales on its sides, to the three minor scales standing below these three major scales, and finally, to the three minor scales standing still farther towards the left. Thus : F♯ major is related to C♯ and to B major, to D♯, A♯, and G♯ minor, and also to C♯, F♯, and B minor.

SECTION VI.

The modulation into any scale outside the circle of relationship, must be effected by means of one or more intermediate scales.

1st.—The modulation into a scale which is but one step outside of the relation, would be too abrupt to be effected without abridgment. Hence, the modulation, *e. g.*, from C major into D major proceeds most naturally by means of the intermediate scale of G major, or of E minor, and from thence into the scale of D major.

From C major into D major, by way of G major :

Degrees in G major: IV   II   V   I
Degrees in D major: IV   II   V   I

From C major into D major, by way of E minor :

Degrees in E minor: VI   II   V   I
   "   " *D major:*   II   V   I

A similar course must always be pursued if a modulation is to be effected from any major scale into the second upon its right. The modulation from C major into B♭ major, proceeds most naturally, first, to the scale of.F major, or of D or G minor, and from thence to that of B♭ major.

From C major into B♭ major, by way of F major:

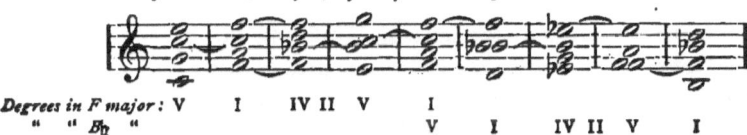

Degrees in F major: V   I   IV II V   I
  "   " *B♭*   "   V   I   IV II V   I

From C major into B♭ major, by way of G minor :

Degrees in G minor: IV   II   V   I
  "   " *B♭ major:*   VI   II   V   I

A like method must always be pursued, if a modulation is to be made from any major scale into the second on its left.

2d.—The modulation from any major scale into the third on its right, admits of one abridgment, *i. e.*, we proceed first to that minor scale which possesses the same first degree with the desired major scale, and is always found immediately below the major scale from which we started. Thus : the modulation from C major into A major is effected by means of A minor, which contains the major triad of C upon its 3d degree. This triad is to be succeeded by the regular fundamental progressions, until the dominant harmony is reached, which affords the best opportunity to close in A major, instead of A minor.

From C major into A major, by way of A minor:

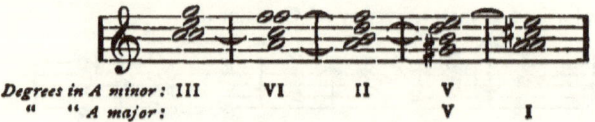

Degrees in A minor: III   VI   II   V
   "   " A major: V   I

The modulation from any major scale into the third on its left finds its abridgment in the treatment of the first chord as dominant triad of the minor scale standing on the left of the desired major scale, the tonic triad of which is obtained by the regular fundamental progressions. Thus: in the modulation from C into E♭ major, the major triad of C is treated as dominant triad of F minor, and succeeded by the tonic triad of that scale. This triad is again treated as that of the 2d degree of E♭ major, whose tonic is reached by the regular fundamental progressions.

From C major into E♭ major, by way of F minor:

Degrees in F minor: V   I
   "   " E♭ major: II   V   I

3d.—The modulation from any major scale into the fourth on its right, may be abridged by treating the first major triad as that of the natural 6th degree of the minor scale next at its right, to be succeeded by the regular fundamental progressions until the dominant harmony is reached, which, being identical in major and minor, affords the best opportunity to conclude with the desired major triad. Thus: in the modulation from C major into E major, the major triad of C is treated as that of the natural 6th degree of E minor, to be succeeded by the regular fundamental progressions, until the dominant harmony of that scale is reached, which may be followed by the tonic triad of E major.

From C major into E major, by way of E minor:

Degrees in E minor: VI   II   V
   "   " E major: V   I

The modulation from any major scale into the fourth on its left may be abridged by treating the first major triad as dominant triad of the minor scale standing immediately below the desired major scale, to be succeeded by its tonic triad. This latter stands upon the 6th degree of the desired major scale, whose tonic triad is reached by the regular fundamental progressions. Thus: in the modulation from C major into A♭ major, the triad of C major is treated as dominant triad of F minor, to be succeeded by the tonic triad of that scale. The triad of F minor is then treated as that of the 6th degree of A♭ major, whose tonic is reached in the usual manner.

From C major into A♭ major, by way of F minor:

Degrees in F minor: V   I
    "   " *A♭ major:*   VI   II   V   I

4th.—The modulation from any major scale into the fifth on its right, needs two abridgments. It leads at first into the major or minor scale on its right; after that, into the minor scale on the right of the latter. The dominant harmony of this last scale being reached, may be succeeded by the major triad of the desired tone. Thus: in the modulation from C major into B major, the major triad of C is treated as that of the 4th degree of G major, or of the natural 6th degree of E minor. After reaching the tonic triad of either of these scales, the modulation leads into B minor, whose dominant harmony may be succeeded by the tonic triad of B major.

From C major into B major, by way of G major and B minor:

Degrees in G major: IV   II   V   I
   "   " *B minor:*   VI   II   V
   "   " *B major:*   V   I

The modulation from any major scale into the fifth on its left, may be effected by treating the first major triad as dominant triad of the fourth minor scale on its left, leading to the tonic triad, which is then treated as triad of the 3d degree of the required major scale, whose tonic is reached as usual. Thus: the modulation from C major into D♭ major leads first into the scale of F minor, whose tonic triad, being treated as triad of the 3d degree of D♭ major, is succeeded by the usual fundamental progressions, until a close is reached.

From C major into D♭ major, by way of F minor:

Degrees in F minor: V   I
   "   " *D♭ major:*   III   VI   II   V   I

5th.—The modulation from any major scale into the sixth on its right, requires two abridgments, viz.: the first major triad is treated as that of the 3d degree of the minor scale standing immediately below, to be succeeded by the usual fundamental progressions, up to its dominant harmony, leading into the major scale of the same name. The tonic triad of this scale is again treated as triad of the 3d degree of the minor scale standing immediately below, to be succeeded by the usual fundamental progressions up to its dominant, leading into the major scale of the same name. Thus: the modulation from C major into F♯ major may be effected by treating the major triad of C as that of the 3d degree of A minor, whose dominant may be succeeded by the major triad of A. This triad being treated as that of the third degree of F♯ minor, is followed by the usual progressions up to the dominant, leading into the major triad of the required scale.

From C major into F♯ major, by way of A minor and F♯ minor:

Degrees in A minor:	III	VI	II	V					
" " A major:				V	I				
" " F♯ minor:						III	VI	II	V
" " F♯ major:								V	I

The modulation from any major scale into the sixth on its left is also abridged twice. The first major triad is treated as dominant of the fourth minor scale on its left, to be succeeded by its tonic. This minor triad is treated as that of the 2d degree of the second minor scale on its left. The tonic triad of this last minor scale is treated as triad of the 6th degree of the desired major scale, whose tonic is reached as usual. Thus: in modulating from C major into G♭ major, we begin by treating the major triad of C as dominant of F minor. The minor triad of F stands upon the 2d degree of E♭ minor, whose tonic is reached as usual. The minor triad of E♭ stands upon the 6th degree of G♭ major, whose tonic is also reached in the usual manner.

From C major into G♭ major, by way of F minor and E♭ minor:

Degrees in F minor:	V	I					
" " E♭ minor:	II	V	I				
" " G♭ major:			VI	II	V	I	

6th.—The modulation from any major scale into the seventh on its right, is abridged twice. The first major triad is treated as that of the natural 6th degree of the minor scale on the right; the dominant of this minor scale, having been reached in the usual way, may be succeeded by the major triad of the same name, which occurs in the table as the fourth one on the right. The new major triad being treated as triad of the 3d degree of the minor scale immediately below, is followed by the usual fundamental progressions, leading into the tonic of the desired major scale. Thus : the modulation from C major into C♯ major begins by treating the major triad of C as that of the natural 6th degree of E minor, whose dominant being reached, is succeeded by the major triad of the same name. The major triad of E, which stands upon the 3d degree of C♯ minor, is followed by the usual fundamental progressions up to the dominant, leading into the major triad of C♯.

From C major into C♯ major, by way of E minor and C♯ minor:

Degrees in E minor:	VI	II	V					
" " E major:			V	I				
" " C♯ minor:				III	VI	II	V	
" " C♯ major:							V	I

The modulation from any major scale into the seventh on its left, is also abridged twice. The first major triad is treated as dominant triad of the fourth minor scale on the left; the tonic triad of this minor scale is then treated as triad of the 2d degree of the 2d minor scale on its left, whose tonic triad stands upon the 3d degree of the required scale. Thus : the modulation from C major to C♭ major begins by treating the major triad of C as dominant of F minor. The minor triad of F is treated as triad of the 2d degree of E♭ minor, the tonic of which stands upon the 3d degree of C♭ major, whose tonic is reached in the usual manner.

From C major into C♭ major, by way of F minor and E♭ minor:

Degrees in F minor:	V	I						
" " E♭ minor:		II	V	I				
" " C♭ major:				III	VI	II	V	I

SECTION VII.

1st.—The modulation from any minor scale into the second on its right, admits of no abridgment, because these two scales are not related. In other respects, this modulation must be effected in the same way as in the concluding examples of Section IV.

. The modulation from any minor scale into the second upon its left, is easily effected, as has been already shown in Section IV.

2d.—To modulate from any minor scale into the third on its right, the tonic triad of the first scale is succeeded by its dominant, which must be treated as triad of the natural 7th degree of the desired minor scale, the tonic of which is reached in the usual manner. Thus : to modulate from A minor into F♯ minor, the minor triad of A is succeeded by its dominant triad, standing in F♯ minor upon the natural 7th degree, to be followed by the regular fundamental progressions, until a close is reached.

From A minor into F♯ minor :

Degrees in A minor :   I   V
  "   " F♯ minor :   VII   III   VI   II   V   I

The dominant triad of A minor may also be considered as dominant of A major, without, however, altering the result, as the tonic triad of A major stands in all cases upon the 3d degree of F♯ minor.

The modulation from any minor scale into the third on its left, is effected by treating the first minor triad as triad of the 2d degree of the major scale on the right, to be followed by its dominant and tonic, which latter is then treated as dominant of the desired scale. Thus : we modulate from A minor to C minor, by treating the minor triad of A as triad of the 2d degree of G major, to be followed by the dominant and tonic of this scale ; the major triad of G is then treated as dominant, to be succeeded by the minor triad of C.

From A minor into C minor :

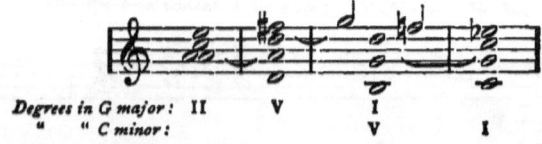

Degrees in G major :   II   V   I
  "   " C minor :   V   I

3d.—To modulate from any minor scale into the fourth on its right, we treat the first minor triad as triad of the 4th degree of the next minor scale on the right, to be succeeded by the regular fundamental progressions up to the dominant, leading into the major triad of that name. This major triad, occurring upon the 3d degree of the desired minor scale, is followed by the regular fundamental progressions, until its tonic is reached. Thus : in modulating from A minor into C♯ minor, we treat the minor triad of A as that of the 4th degree of E minor, which is then succeeded by the usual progressions, leading into E major. The major triad of E, being treated as that of the 3d degree of C♯ minor, is followed by the regular fundamental progressions, until its tonic is reached.

From A minor into C♯ minor, by way of E minor and E major:

Degrees in E minor:	IV	II	V						
" " E *major:*			V	I					
" " C♯ *minor:*				I	III	VI	II	V	I

To modulate from any minor scale into the fourth on its left, we treat the first minor triad as that of the 6th degree of the major scale standing immediately above. The tonic triad of this scale, having been reached as usual, is treated as dominant of the desired scale, to be succeeded by its tonic. Thus: in modulating from A minor into F minor, we treat the minor triad of A as that of the 6th degree of C major, whose tonic triad is reached as usual, and treated as dominant of F minor, after which the minor triad of F may follow.

From A minor into F minor, by way of C major:

Degrees in C major:	VI	II	V		
" " F *minor:*			V	I	

4th.—In modulating from any minor scale into the fifth on its right, we treat the first minor triad as that of the 4th degree of the next minor scale on the right, which, being succeeded by the regular fundamental progressions up to its dominant, leads into the major scale of that name. The tonic triad of this scale is treated as triad of the natural 6th degree of the desired minor scale, whose tonic is reached as usual. Thus: in modulating from A minor into G♯ minor, we treat the minor triad of A as that of the 4th degree of E minor, to be succeeded by the regular fundamental progressions, leading into E major. The major triad of E is then treated as that of the natural 6th degree of G♯ minor, whose tonic is reached as usual.

From A minor into G♯ minor, by way of E minor and E major:

Degrees in E minor:	IV	II	V				
" " E *major:*			V	I			
" " G♯ *minor:*				VI	II	V	I

In modulating from any minor scale into the fifth on its left, we treat the first minor triad as that of the 3d degree of the major scale on the left, whose tonic triad, being reached in the usual manner, is treated as dominant of the desired minor scale. Thus : in modulating from A minor into B♭ minor, we treat the minor triad of A as that of the 3d degree of F major, whose tonic is reached as usual, and treated as dominant of B♭ minor, to be succeeded by the tonic of the desired scale.

From A minor into B♭ minor, by way of F major :

Degrees in F major : III   VI   II   V   I
"   " B♭ minor: V   I

5th.—To modulate from any minor scale into the sixth on its right, we treat the first minor triad as that of the 4th degree of the next minor scale on the right, which, being followed by the regular fundamental progressions, leads into the major scale of that name. The major triad of this scale may be treated as triad either of the 4th degree of the major scale on its right, or of the natural 6th degree of the minor scale on its right. From the tonic of either of these scales, the desired scale is easily reached. Thus : in modulating from A minor into D♯ minor, we treat the minor triad of A as that of the 4th degree of E minor, to be succeeded by the regular fundamental progressions, leading into E major. The major triad of E is then treated as that of the 4th degree of B major, or as that of the natural 6th degree of G♯ minor, the first standing upon the natural 6th, and the latter upon the 4th degree of D♯ minor, whose tonic is reached in the usual manner.

From A minor into D♯ minor, by means of E minor and B major :

Degrees in E minor : IV   II   V
"   " E major: V   I
"   " B major: IV   II   V   I
"   " D♯ minor: VI   II   V   I

To modulate from any minor scale into the sixth on its left, we treat the first minor triad as that of the 6th degree of the major scale standing immediately above, to be followed by the regular fundamental progressions up to its tonic. The tonic triad of this scale is then treated as dominant of the fourth minor scale on its left, to be followed by its tonic, which is treated as triad of the 2d degree of the desired scale, whose tonic is reached in the usual manner. Thus : in modulating from A minor into E♭ minor, we treat the minor triad of A as that of the 6th degree of C major, whose tonic is reached as usual, to be treated as dominant of F minor. The minor triad of F is treated as that of the 2d degree of E♭ minor, whose tonic is reached as usual.

From A minor into E♭ minor, by way of C major and F minor:

Degrees in C major:	VI	II	V	I			
" " F minor:				V	I		
" " E♭ minor:					II	V	I

6th.—In modulating from any minor scale into the seventh on its right, we treat the first minor triad as that of the 4th degree of the next minor scale on the right, which, being succeeded by the regular fundamental progressions, leads into the major scale of that name. The tonic triad of this scale is treated as triad of the 3d degree of the minor scale immediately below, to be followed by the regular fundamental progressions, leading into the major scale of that name. The tonic triad of this scale is then treated as triad of the 3d degree of the desired minor scale, whose tonic is reached as usual. Thus: in modulating from A minor into A♯ minor, we treat the minor triad of A as that of the 4th degree of E minor, to be succeeded by the regular fundamental progressions, leading into E major. The major triad of E is then treated as triad of the 3d degree of C♯ minor, to be followed by the regular fundamental progressions, leading into C♯ major. The major triad of C♯ is treated as triad of the 3d degree of A♯ minor, whose tonic is reached as usual.

From A minor into A♯ minor, by way of E minor and C♯ minor:

Deg. in E minor:	IV	II	V							
" " E major:			V	I						
" " C♯ minor:				III	VI	II	V			
" " C♯ major:							V	I		
" " A♯ minor:								III	VI	II	V	I

In modulating from any minor scale into the seventh on its left, we treat the first minor triad as that of the 3d degree of the next major scale on the left, to be succeeded by the regular fundamental progressions until its tonic is reached. The tonic triad of this scale is then treated as dominant triad of the fourth minor scale at its left, to be followed by its tonic. This last minor triad is treated as that of the 2d degree of the desired scale, whose tonic is reached as usual. Thus: in modulating from A minor into Ab minor, we treat the minor triad of A as that of the 3d degree of F major, to be succeeded by the regular fundamental progressions, till the tonic is reached. The major triad of F is then treated as dominant triad of Bb minor, to be followed by the tonic of that scale. The minor triad of Bb is treated as that of the 2d degree of Ab minor, whose tonic is reached as usual.

From A minor into Ab minor, by way of F major and Bb minor:

Degrees in F major: III   VI   II   V   I
    " " Bb minor: V   I .
    " " Ab minor: II   V   I

SECTION VIII.

In the table, in Section V, we notice that the scale of C# major has no step to its right, and that the scale of Cb major has none to the left. The scale of F# major has but one step to its right, and that of Gb major, but one step to its left, etc.

The modulation from Cb major into C# major may be effected in four progressions, viz.: 1st, from Cb major into Eb major, by means of Eb minor; 2d, from Eb major into C major, by means of C minor; 3d, from C major into E major, by means of E minor; and 4th, from E major into C# major, by means of C# minor.

The modulation from C# major into Cb major may be effected in six (shorter) progressions, viz.: 1st, from C# major into F# minor; 2d, from F# minor into E minor; 3d, from E minor into C major; 4th, from C major into F minor; 5th, from F minor into Eb minor; and 6th, from Eb minor into Cb major: or, 1st, from C# major into F# minor; 2d, from F# minor into D major; 3d, from D major into G minor; 4th, from G minor into Eb major; 5th, from Eb major into Ab minor; and 6th, from Ab minor into Cb major.

The modulation from Ab minor into A# minor may be effected in five progressions, viz.: 1st, from Ab minor into Eb major, by means of Eb minor; 2d, from Eb major into G major, by means of G minor; 3d, from G major into E major, by means of E minor; 4th, from E major into C# major, by means of C# minor; and 5th, from C# major into A# minor.

The modulation from A# minor into Ab minor may be effected in six progressions, viz.: 1st, from A# minor into F# major; 2d, from F# major into B minor; 3d, from B minor into G major; 4th, from G major into

C minor ; 5th, from C minor into E♭ major ; and 6th, from E♭ major into A♭ minor.

All these modulations should be practised with primary chords, as well as with their inversions.

SECTION IX.

The *close* to which a modulation tends, which, for our present purpose, we will call its *resolution*, may be accelerated by contraction (use of substitute chords), of which examples have been already given, in connection with the discussion of the major and minor scales. The following examples of contraction are recommended as the most practical.

1st.—The triad of the 4th degree requires the succession of the harmony of the 2d degree, if the dominant harmony is desired. But the triad of the 4th degree may be succeeded directly by the dominant harmony, if the former is treated as substitute for the chord of the seventh of the 2d degree.

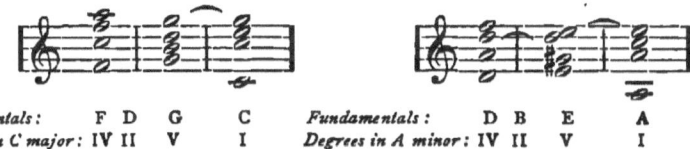

| *Fundamentals:* | F | D | G | | C |
| *Degrees in C major:* | IV | II | V | | I |

| *Fundamentals:* | D | B | E | | A |
| *Degrees in A minor:* | IV | II | V | | I |

2d.—The triad of the 6th degree must also be followed by the harmony of the 2d degree, if the dominant harmony is to be reached. But the triad of the 6th degree (or rather its first inversion) may be succeeded directly by the dominant harmony, if it is treated as substitute for the chord of the seventh and ninth of the 2d degree.

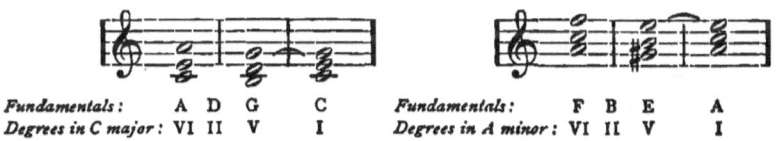

| *Fundamentals:* | A | D | G | | C |
| *Degrees in C major:* | VI | II | V | | I |

| *Fundamentals:* | F | B | E | | A |
| *Degrees in A minor:* | VI | II | V | | I |

3d.—The triad of the 3d degree of the major scale may be succeeded directly by the dominant harmony.

| *Fundamentals:* | E | G | C |
| *Degrees in C major:* | III | V | I |

4th.—The major triad of the 3d degree of the minor scale may be succeeded directly by the diminished harmony of the 2d degree, if the former is treated as substitute for the chord of the seventh and ninth of the natural 6th degree.

Fundamentals: C   F   B   E   A
Degrees in A minor: III VI   II   V   I

5th.—The triad of the natural 7th degree of the minor scale may be considered as dependent, if it occurs without octave. In this case, that tone which otherwise would be fundamental, may be treated as thirteenth of the of the 2d degree ; as such it may resolve one degree downward, while the other tones remain, thereby producing the harmony of the 2d degree, which may be succeeded by that of the dominant.

Fundamentals: B.........   E   A
Degrees in A minor: II.........   V   I

SECTION X.

The resolution of a modulation may also be delayed, by progressions of the following kind :

1st.—The dominant harmony may be followed by the tonic ; the succession of the harmony of the *3d degree* delays the resolution.

2d.—The harmony of the 2d may be followed by that of the 5th degree ; the succession of that of the *7th degree* delays the resolution.

3d.—The harmony of the 6th may be followed by that of the 2d degree ; the succession of the harmony of the *4th*, of the *1st*, or of the *3d degree*, delays the resolution.

4th.—The harmony of the 3d is followed most naturally by that of the 6th degree ; the succession of the harmony of the *1st degree* effects no close, as this must be reached by the usual fundamental progressions.

5th.—The triad of the 4th is followed by the harmony of the 2d degree, if a direct close is intended ; but this close will be delayed, if the triad of the 4th is followed by that of the *6th* or *1st* degree, or by the harmony of the *7th* degree.

SECTION XI.

If, of two periods, one closes with one tonic, while the succeeding one begins with another, the passage is best effected in accordance with the laws of natural relationship, as shown in the following scheme :

a. If the first period ends with a major triad, the new period properly begins with the major triad of its perfect upper or under-fifth, or with the minor triad of its major upper-third, or of its minor under-third, or of its perfect under-fifth. In other words : the concluding triad of the first period must stand upon the 4th or 5th degree of the new major scale, or upon the 3d, or 5th, or 6th degree of the new minor scale. For example : the first period having closed with the major triad of C, the second may begin with the major triad of G or F, or with the minor triad of A, E, or F.

b. If the first period closes with a minor triad, the new period begins most naturally with the minor triad of its perfect upper or under-fifth, or with the major triad of its minor upper-third, or of its major under-third, or of its perfect upper-fifth. In other words : the concluding triad of the first period must stand upon the 4th or 5th degree of the new minor scale, or upon the 6th or 3d degree of the new major scale. The last triad occurs only upon the 5th degree of the first minor scale. For example : the first period having closed with the minor triad of A, the second period may begin with the minor triad of D or E, or with the major triad of C, F, or E.

Hence we conclude, that the succession of two triads, each of which is to represent a tonic, must be regarded as a regular fundamental progression.

What course is to be pursued in the case of two periods, respectively closing and beginning with a major and minor triad *on the same degree*, will be self-evident when the explanation of chromatic progressions is fully comprehended.

SECTION XII.

We have had, in this part of our treatise, but one object in view, viz.: to show how much may be effected by means of *diatonic modulation* alone, and to prove that this species is not merely an apparent, but a real modulation, enabling us to recognize every tonic triad as such, at any time, and under all circumstances.

We conclude with the remark, that the species of modulation explained in this part, is founded on the tempered system—a circumstance which, however, places no difficulties in the way of effecting the harmonic successions in exact conformity with the rules laid down in Parts I and II of this treatise.

PART IV.

CHROMATIC PROGRESSIONS IN THE SCALE OF C MAJOR.

SECTION I.

IF, between two tones of a diatonic scale which are distant a major second, a tone of a *relative key* is inserted, we have a *chromatic progression.* The keys related to C major, our normal scale, are : G major, F major, A minor, E minor, D minor, G minor, C minor, and F minor.

The insertions in the *ascending* scale take place as follows :

Between *c* and *d* we place *c♯*, from the scale of *D minor*, which also contains *c* and *d*.

Between *d* and *e* we place *d♯*, from the scale of *E minor*, which also contains *d* and *e*.

Between *f* and *g* we place *f♯*, from the scale of either *G major* or *G minor*, which latter also contains *f* and *g*.

Between *g* and *a* we place *g♯*, from the scale of *A minor*, which also contains *g* and *a*.

Between *a* and *b* we place *b♭*, from the scale of either *F major, D minor,* or *C minor*, the last two of which also contain *a* and *b*.

Descending.—Between *b* and *a* we place *b♭*, from the scales of *F major, D minor* and *C minor*, the latter two of which also contain *b* and *a*.

Between *a* and *g* we place *a♭*, from the scale of *C minor*, which also contains *a* and *g*.

Between *g* and *f* we place *f♯*, from the scale of *G major* or *G minor*, which latter also contains *g* and *f*.

Between *e* and *d* we place *e♭*, from the scale of *G minor*, which also contains *e* and *d*.

Between *d* and *c* we place *d♭*, from the scale of *F minor*, which also contains *d* and *c*.

REMARK.—We distinguish, moreover, periods artificially related, in which the insertions, descending, are effected thus : *g♯* is placed **between** *a* and *g ; d♯* between *e* and *d*, and *c♯* between *e* and *d*.

SECTION II.

A careful examination of Section I will show that the relative minor scales furnish most of the means for chromatic progressions, owing to the fact that the 6th and 7th degrees of the diatonic minor scale succeed each other *raised*, in *ascending*, and *natural*, in *descending ;* whilst, in chromatic progression, each of these degrees may successively appear *in both forms.*

In the diatonic scale of A minor, the ascending degrees, 5, 6, 7 and 8 are, *e, f♯, g♯, a ;* those descending from the 8th to the 5th degree are, *a, g, f, e.* In chromatic progressions they are intermingled in the following manner : *e, f, f♯, g, g♯, a ;* descending in reversed order.

In the diatonic scale of E minor, the ascending degrees from the 5th to the 8th, are, *b, c♯, d♯, e ;* those descending from the 8th to the 5th are, *e, d, c, b.* The intermingling of these will give the chromatic progressions, *b, c, c♯, d, d♯, e ;* descending in reversed order.

In the diatonic scale of D minor, the ascending degrees from the 5th to the 8th are, *a, b, c♯, d ;* those descending from the 8th to the 5th are, *d, c, b♭, a.* The intermingling of these gives the chromatic progressions, *a, b♭, b♮, c, c♯, d ;* descending in reversed order.

The examination of these three minor scales enables us to understand the nature of the *ascending chromatic scale* of C major, since it is of their component tones that this scale is made up, viz.: *c, c♯, d, d♯, e, f, f♯, g, g♯, a, b♭, b♮, c.*

The diatonic scale of C minor ascends from the 5th to the 8th degree : *g, a, b, c,* and descends from the 8th to the 5th : *c, b♭, a♭, g.* These being intermingled give the chromatic progressions : *g, a♭, a♮, b♭, b♮, c,* descending in reversed order.

The diatonic scale of G minor ascends from the 5th to the 8th degree : *d, e, f♯, g ;* and descends from the 8th to the 5th : *g, f, e♭, d.* These being intermingled give the chromatic progressions ; *d, e♭, e♮, f, f♯, g ;* descending in reversed order.

The diatonic scale of F minor ascends from the 5th to the 8th degree : *c, d, e, f,* and descends from the 8th to the 5th : *f, e♭, d♭, c.* These being intermingled give the chromatic progressions : *c, d♭, d♮, e♭, e♮, f ;* descending in reversed order.

The examination of the last three minor scales enables us to understand the nature of the *descending chromatic scale* of C major, since it is of their component tones that this scale is made up, viz.: *c, b, b♭, a, a♭, g, f♯, f♮, e, e♭, d, d♭, c.*

SECTION III.

The use of the chromatic tones cannot be extended to fundamentals. The chromatic scale of C major, therefore, has no other fundamentals than the diatonic, viz.: the diatonic degrees, C, D, E, F, G, A, and B, which may be treated for a short time as degrees of a relative scale, thus :

I. The tones, C, F, D, G, may be treated as the same degrees in C major and C minor, that is, in both as the 1st, 4th, 2d and 5th degrees.

II. The tones, D, G, E, A, 2d, 5th, 3d and 6th degrees in C major, may be treated as 1st, 4th, 2d and 5th degrees in D minor.

III. The tones, E, A, B, 3d, 6th and 7th degrees in C major, may be treated as 1st, 4th and 5th degrees in E minor.

IV. The tones, F, G, C, 4th, 5th and 1st degrees in C major, may be treated as 1st, 2d and 5th degrees in F major, or F minor.

V. The tones, G, C, A, D, 5th, 1st, 6th and 2d degrees in C major, may be treated as 1st, 4th, 2d and 5th degrees in G major, or G minor.

VI. The tones, A, D, B, E, 6th, 2d, 7th and 3d degrees in C major, may be treated as 1st, 4th, 2d and 5th degrees in A minor.

SECTION IV.

I. The triad of the 1st degree of the scale of C major may be altered into that of the 1st degree of C minor by changing its major third, e, into a minor third, $e\flat$. It needs no alteration to stand as triad of the 5th degree of F major, or F minor, unless the minor triad of the latter is required. It needs no alteration to stand as triad of the 4th degree of G major, but its major third must be altered into a minor third, if it is to stand as characteristic triad of the 4th degree of G minor. Its change into the characteristic triad of the 3d degree of A minor is effected by the alteration of its perfect fifth, g, into an augmented fifth, $g\sharp$. It needs no alteration to stand as triad of the natural 6th degree of E minor, or (in the tempered system) of the natural 7th degree of D minor.

The triad of the 1st degree of C major cannot by right be altered into that of the 2d degree of B♭ major, nor into that of the 6th degree of E♭ major, because $b\flat$ and $e\flat$ are not diatonic tones in C major, and therefore cannot stand as fundamentals of that scale.

II. The triad of the 2d degree of C major (in the tempered system) needs no alteration to stand as triad of the 1st degree of D minor. Its change into the triad of the 5th degree of G major or G minor depends upon the alteration of its minor third, f, into a major third, $f\sharp$. It needs no alteration (in the tempered system) to stand as minor triad of the 4th degree of A minor, or of the 6th degree of F major. Its alteration into the characteristic triad of the 2d degree of C minor is effected by the change of its (dubious) fifth, a, into a diminished fifth, $a\flat$.

III. The triad of the 3d degree of C major needs no alteration to stand as triad of the 1st degree of E minor, or as that of the 6th degree of G major. Its alteration into the characteristic triad of the 5th degree of A minor, is effected by the change of its minor third, g, into a major third, $g\sharp$. Its alteration into the characteristic triad of the 2d degree of D minor, or of the 7th degree of F major, is effected by the change of the perfect fifth, b, into a diminished fifth, $b\flat$.

IV. The triad of the 4th degree of C major needs no alteration to stand as triad of the 1st degree of F major, or of the natural 6th degree of A minor. Its change into the triad of the 1st degree of F minor, or into the characteristic triad of the 4th degree of C minor, is effected by altering its major third, a, into a minor third, $a\flat$. Its change into the characteristic triad of the 3d degree of D minor, is effected by the alteration of its perfect fifth, c, into an augmented fifth, $c\sharp$. It needs no alteration (in the tempered system) to stand as triad of the natural 7th degree of G minor. It cannot be treated as the triad of the 5th degree of B$\flat$ major, nor be altered into the triad of the 2d degree of E$\flat$ major, or of the 6th degree of A$\flat$ major, because $b\flat$, $e\flat$ and $a\flat$ are not diatonic tones of C major, and therefore, cannot occur as fundamentals of that scale.

V. The triad of the 5th degree of C major needs no alteration to become the triad of the 1st degree of G major, nor of the 5th degree of C minor, unless the minor triad of the 5th degree of C minor is required, which is obtained by the alteration of the major third, b, into a minor third, $b\flat$. Its change into the triad of the 1st degree of G minor, or of the 2d degree of F major, or of the 4th degree of D minor, is also effected by the alteration of the major third, b, into a minor third, $b\flat$. Its alteration into the characteristic triad of the 2d degree of F minor is effected by the change of the major third into a minor third, and by that of the perfect fifth, d, into a diminished fifth, $d\flat$. Its change into the characteristic triad of the 3d degree of E minor, is effected by the alteration of its perfect fifth, d, into an augmented fifth, $d\sharp$.

VI. The triad of the 6th degree of C major needs no change to stand as triad of the 1st degree of A minor, or of the 3d degree of F major, or of the 4th degree of E minor. It also needs no alteration (in the tempered system) to stand as triad of the 2d degree of G major. Its change into the characteristic triad of the 2d degree of G minor is effected by altering its perfect fifth, e, into a diminished fifth, $e\flat$. Its alteration into the characteristic triad of the 5th degree of D minor, is effected by the change of its minor third, c, into a major third, $c\sharp$.

VII. The triad of the 7th degree of C major cannot become a triad of the 1st, 5th, 4th or 3d degree of a relative scale, because its diminished fifth cannot be altered into a perfect fifth.   Hence it can be treated only as triad of the 2d degree of A minor, as triad of the raised 6th degree of D minor, and as triad of the raised 7th degree of C minor.

These observations sufficiently explain the mode of alteration also of the *chords of the seventh,* and of the *seventh and ninth,* of each degree in the scale of C major, with special reference to their occurrence in a relative scale. We will only add, that *major* sevenths or ninths may be altered into *minor* sevenths or ninths, but not *vice versa.*

In the chromatic alterations of chords of the seventh, and of the seventh and ninth, when in the former the third and seventh, and in the latter the fifth and ninth are to be lowered, it is better that the change effecting a nearer, should precede that effecting a more distant relationship.

Whenever, in a chromatically altered chord of the seventh, a simultaneous resolution of the minor third and minor seventh is intended (*e. g.,* by means of the ascent of the fundamentals by degrees), care must be taken to place the minor third above the seventh ; otherwise, consecutive fifths would result.

For the same reason, *i. e.,* to avoid consecutive fifths, the diminished fifth of a chromatically altered chord of the seventh and ninth must stand above the ninth, whenever their simultaneous resolution is intended.

SECTION V.

The case of *different triads upon the same fundamental,* is best explained by the consideration of the several minor scales.

Both the major and the minor triad of C stand upon the 4th degree of G minor, and upon the 5th of F minor.

Both the major and the augmented triad of C stand upon the 3d degree of A minor.

Both the minor and the major triad of D stand upon the 4th degree of A minor, and upon the 5th of G minor.

Both the minor and the diminished triad of D stand upon the 2d degree of C minor.

Both the minor and the major triad of E stand upon the 5th degree of A minor.

Both the minor and the diminished triad of E stand upon the 2d degree of D minor.

Both the major and the minor triad of F stand upon the 4th degree of C minor.

Both the major and the augmented triad of F stand upon the 3d degree of D minor.

Both the major and the minor triad of G stand upon the 4th degree of D minor, and upon the 5th of C minor.

Both the minor and the diminished triad of G stand upon the 2d degree of F minor.

Both the major and the augmented triad of G stand upon the 3d degree of E minor.

Both the minor and the major triad of A stand upon the 4th degree of of E minor, and upon the 5th of D minor.

Both the minor and the diminished triad of A stand upon the 2d degree of G minor.

SECTION VI.

Alterations of diatonic into chromatic tones, and *vice versa*, must be made in the same voice, otherwise, harsh and faulty progressions will result, *e. g.*:

A faulty progression of this nature is termed *false relation*, and is avoided in the following way :

If it be asked, whether this false relation still exists, if the chromatic alteration takes place with an exchange of tones of the same fundamental, such exchange being connected by the intermediate passing tones, *e. g.*:

we maintain, that even in this case the false relation still exists.

But there are other progressions, seemingly involving the false relation, yet perfectly legitimate, viz.:

1st.—Progressions which occur during the continuance of the same fundamental, by means of chromatic changing notes, *e. g.*:

2d.—Progressions which occur, if two voices sound the same tone of a chord ; in which case, both voices may progress chromatically in contrary motion, *e. g.*:

3d.—Progressions which occur if the chromatic alteration takes place at the end and at the beginning of a passage ; provided the altered tone causing the false relation does not occur in the two upper or in the two outer voices, *e. g.*:

SECTION VII.

Every chromatic harmony should be founded upon a diatonic harmony. How chromatic progressions arise from a diatonic passage, will be exemplified hereafter.

It should also be mentioned in this place, that in those examples in which the fundamentals are found in the lowest voice, the usual indications of the fundamentals will be omitted ; and that in those examples in which *inversions* occur, the fundamentals will be indicated by capital letters.

SECTION VIII.

The returning motion of each component tone of any triad of the diatonic major scale, is effected by means of *chromatic steps, i. e.,* we raise or lower that tone which is to be reached by the returning motion; provided the tone thus altered is a diatonic tone of some relative scale.

The following examples will illustrate the returning motions of the component tones of the tonic triad of C major.

The progression at (*d*) is preferable to that at (*c*), as *f*♯ more naturally returns to *g* than *f*♮.

The progression at (*h*) is not good, because it is more natural for *f*♯ to ascend to *g*, than to return to *e*.

In the above two examples, the *chromatic alterations* indicate the *dominant* harmony of F minor and F major.

SECTION IX.

1st.—The chromatic steps arising from the descent of the fundamental by a fifth, or its ascent by a fourth:

An exemplification of the chromatic progression from the diminished triad of the 7th to the minor triad of the 3d degree, is involved in Section XVI.

2d.—The chromatic steps arising from the ascent of the fundamental by a fifth, or its descent by a fourth:

3d.—The chromatic steps arising from the descent of the fundamental by a third:

The last examples may also occur with passing tones, and returning motions, *e. g.*:

Fund. C........ A   F........ D   G........ E

4th.—When the fundamental ascends by a third, chromatic steps are not conceivable.

5th.—With regard to the seeming ascent of the fundamental by degrees, it may be observed, that if the first chord contains two minor thirds of the tacit fundamental, one of them may step to the major third, and the other to the minor ninth, *e g.*:

Fund. C A D   C   A   D   C   A   D C   A   D C   A   D

C♯ and *b♮* are component parts of the dominant chord of the seventh and ninth of D minor.

Fund. D B E   D   B   E

Fund. F D G   F   D   G

F♯ and *e♮* are component parts of the dominant harmony of G minor.

Fund. G E A   G   E   A

G♯ and *f* are component parts of the dominant harmony of A minor.

Fund. E C F   E   C   F   E   C   F

B♭ and *d♭* are component parts of the dominant harmony of F minor.

F♯ from G minor is reached by returning motion.

The following examples will illustrate other chromatic steps arising from the seeming ascent of fundamentals by degrees:

In the succession of the chord of the seventh of the 6th degree and the triad of the 7th degree, of the scale of C major, the former must be treated as substitute for the chord of the seventh and ninth of the 4th degree. This progression can be chromatically altered only by a license, which we may explain thus: The triad of the 4th degree cannot become a triad of the 2d degree (see Section IV, ɪv), whilst the triad of the 7th degree cannot become one of the 5th degree (See Section IV, vɪɪ). But since the above-mentioned succession introduces the 4th degree only as tacit fundamental, the license of treating *f♯* as such, instead of *f♮*, may be made use of, and *f♯* may be treated as standing upon the 2d degree of E minor. The succeeding triad of *b* may then stand as dominant triad of E minor, leading into the tonic triad of that scale, *e. g.:*

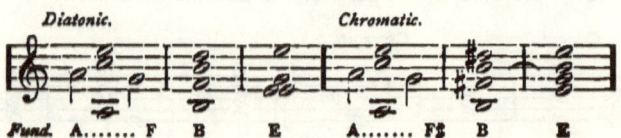

6th.—The chromatic steps arising from the seeming descent of the funda-mental by degrees :

The diatonic harmonies of the 4th and 3d degrees, and of the 7th and 6th degrees of the major scale, cannot be connected by chromatic progressions.

SECTION X.

When any harmony (triad, chord of the seventh, or chord of the seventh and ninth) is followed by a triad whose fundamental is a fifth lower, such harmony may be treated as standing upon the 5th, and the triad as standing upon the 1st degree of a relative scale ; provided the component tones of the former are altered accordingly, and that the latter consists of a major or minor third, and perfect fifth of diatonic tones.

A dominant harmony succeeded by a major third of diatonic tones, may also be considered as arising from a minor scale, if its major ninth is altered into a minor ninth, thus:

1st.—The harmony of the 1st degree of C major may be treated as dominant harmony of F major, or F minor, and the succeeding fundamental as tonic of F major:

2d.—The harmony of the 2d degree of C major may be treated (in the tempered system) as dominant harmony of G major, or G minor, and the succeeding triad of the 5th degree of C major as tonic triad of G major:

3d.—The harmony of the 3d degree of C major may be treated as dominant harmony of A minor, and the succeeding triad of the 6th degree of C major, as tonic triad of A minor:

4th.—The harmony of the 4th degree of C major cannot be treated as a dominant harmony (vide Section IV, iv).

5th.—The harmony of the 5th degree of C major may be treated as dominant harmony of C minor, if its major ninth is altered into a minor ninth; but it must be succeeded by the major triad of C:

6th.—The harmony of the 6th degree of C major may be treated as dominant harmony of D minor, if it is succeeded by the triad of the 2d degree of C major.

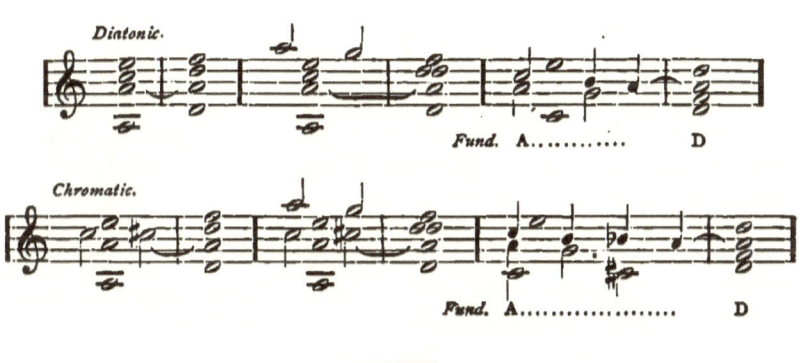

SECTION XI.

In any cadence-like succession (involving fundamental descents by fifths) of two chords of the seventh and a triad, the first chord of the seventh may be treated as that of the 2d degree, the second as that of the 5th degree, and the triad as that of the 1st degree of a relative scale, provided this triad consists of a minor or major third and a perfect fifth, and contains no other but diatonic tones of the first major scale. Thus:

1st.—The chords of the seventh of the 2d and 5th degrees in C major, may be treated as those of the same degrees in C minor, and be resolved into C major:

2d.—The chords of the seventh of the 6th and 2d degrees in C major, may be treated as those of the 2d and 5th degrees of G major, or G minor, and be resolved into G major :

3d.—The chords of the seventh of the 3d and 6th degrees in C major, may be treated as those of the 2d and 5th degrees of D minor, and be resolved into D minor :

4th.—The chords of the seventh of the 7th and 3d degrees in C major, may be treated as those of the 2d and 5th degrees of A minor, and be resolved into A minor :

5th.—The chords of the seventh of the 5th and 1st degrees in C major, may be treated as those of the 2d and 5th degrees of F major or F minor, and be resolved into F major :

The following examples will show that the above explained chromatic progressions are related to the scale of C major :

SECTION XII.

Whenever a chord of the seventh (or triad, or chord of the seventh and ninth) is treated as standing upon the 2d degree of a relative scale, it should be succeeded by the dominant harmony of the same scale, to be resolved into its tonic triad, as explained in the last Section. But if, instead of a triad, a *chord of the seventh* follows (on the same degree), the preceding dominant chord of the seventh should be altered into a chord of the seventh of the 2d degree, by changing the major into a minor third, or by altering the perfect into a diminished fifth. The next chord of the seventh must then be altered into a dominant chord of the seventh, after which it is succeeded by that tonic triad which is the natural resolution of the last chord of the seventh.

The succession of *three chords of the seventh* and a triad in cadence-like order, may be explained thus :

1st.—If, in the succession of the chords of the seventh of the 6th, 2d and 5th degrees, and the triad of the 1st degree, of C major, we treat the first chord of the seventh as that of the 2d degree in G major, or if we alter it into that of the 2d degree in G minor; the succeeding (second) chord of the seventh should be made the dominant harmony of these scales; but since this last chord of the seventh is not succeeded by the tonic triad of G, but by another chord of the seventh, it follows that the dominant harmony of G major should be so altered as to stand for a chord of the seventh of the 2d degree of C major, or C minor. The last (third) chord of the seventh must become a *dominant* chord of the seventh, and resolve into the tonic triad of C major:

2d.—The chords of the seventh of the 3d, 6th and 2d, and the triad of the 5th degree, of C major, may be treated as those of the 6th, 2d, 5th and 1st degrees in G minor and G major:

3d.—The chords of the seventh of the 7th, 3d and 6th, and the triad of the 2d degree, of C major, may be treated as those of the 6th, 2d, 5th and 1st degrees in D minor:

4th.—The chords of the seventh of the 2d, 5th and 1st, and the triad of the 4th degree, of C major, may be treated as those of the 6th, 2d, 5th and 1st degrees in F minor, or F major:

The following succession of the chords of the seventh will sufficiently show the relationship of all these chromatic steps to the scale of C major:

SECTION XIII.

Since the dominant chords of the seventh may enter free and unprepared, it is not necessary to alter any of them into chords of the seventh of the 2d degree. Consequently, the chords of the seventh of the 3d, 6th, 2d, 5th, and 1st degrees, may be altered into the dominant chords of A minor, D minor, G major or G minor, C major and F major. In this manner, all minor sevenths may enter freely together with major thirds, *e. g.*:

By means of the suspension of the ninth, the progressions in the last two examples may be altered thus :

The minor ninth, instead of resolving into the octave of the same funda-mental, may resolve into the perfect fifth of the following fundamental, simultaneously with the entrance of the minor seventh and major third; in this case, the fundamental tone is best omitted.

SECTION XIV.

The harmonies of two successive chords of the seventh, the fundamen-tal of the second being a minor third below that of the first, may be treated as occurring upon the natural 7th and 5th degrees of a relative minor scale. In this case, the seventh of the first chord may be treated as ninth of the second, to resolve into the octave of the second fundamental. Thus, *e. g.:* if the harmony of the chord of the seventh of the 1st degree in C major is followed by that of the 6th degree, the former may be treated as the harmony of the chord of the ninth of the latter degree, the ninth to resolve during the continuance of the same fundamental, after which the triad of the 2d degree may follow. But the fundamental, C, may also be treated as natural 7th degree in D minor, and its seventh, *b*, be altered accordingly into *b♭*, and the succeeding fundamental, A, may be treated as that of the 5th degree in the same scale, by altering the third, *c*, into *c♯*; the triad following may then stand as tonic triad of D minor.

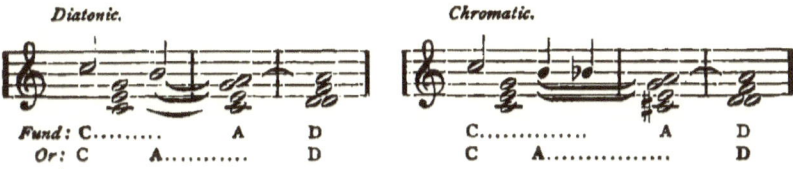

This last example shows that the dominant chord of the seventh in F major is treated as the chord of the seventh and ninth of the 5th degree in D minor, the minor third of which becomes a major third, simultaneously with the resolution of the ninth into the octave.

The treatment will be similar in analogous cases, *e. g.*, in C major, if the harmony of the chord of the seventh of the 4th is followed by that of the 2d degree—F and D being treated as natural 7th and 5th degrees in G minor and G major: and again, if the harmony of the chord of the seventh of the 5th is succeeded by that of the 3d degree—G and E being treated as natural 7th and 5th degrees in A minor. These cases may be illustrated thus:

The same example, with chromatic alterations:

SECTION XV.

The progressions given in the last Section may be treated as occurring upon the 4th and 2d degrees of a relative scale. Thus, *e. g.*, in C major, if the harmony of the chord of the seventh of the 1st is followed by that of the 6th degree, they may be treated as occurring, the former, upon the 4th, and the latter, upon the 2d degree, in G major, to be succeeded by the chord of the seventh of the 5th, and the triad of the 1st degree.

The following chromatic alterations may be made in the above progression, with a view to indicate a relationship to the scale of G minor:

The treatment will be similar in the following analogous cases, *e. g.*, in C major:

1st.—If the harmony of the chord of the seventh of the 2d is succeeded by that of the 7th degree, they may be treated as occurring, the former upon the 4th, and the latter upon the 2d degree, in A minor, to be followed by the dominant and tonic triads, respectively.

2d.—If the harmony of the chord of the seventh of the 4th is succeeded by that of the 2d degree, both may be treated as occurring on the same degrees in C minor, to be followed by the dominant and tonic triads of C major.

3d.—If the harmony of the chord of the seventh of the 5th is succeeded by that of the 3d degree, they may be treated as occurring, the former, upon the 4th, and the latter upon the 2d degree of D minor, to be followed by the dominant and tonic triads of that scale.

The following examples illustrate the relationship of all these chromatic progressions to the scale of C major:

| Fund: C.......... | | A | D | G.......... | | E | A | D.......... | |
| Or: C | A......... | | D | G | E.......... | | A | D | B.... |

| | B | E | A | F.... | D | G | C |
| | .... | E | A | F | D...... | G | C |

The same, with chromatic alterations :

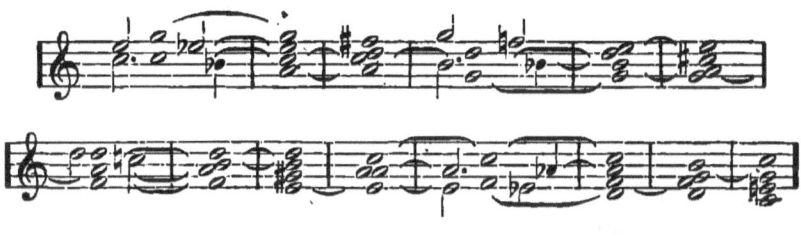

SECTION XVI.

A chord of the seventh (or seventh and ninth), treated as that of the 2d degree of a· relative minor scale, must be composed of a minor third, a diminished fifth, and a minor seventh (minor ninth). By altering the minor into a *major* third, without altering the diminished fifth, a chord is formed whose major third occurs in another scale than that which contains the diminished fifth, because the major third places the chord upon the 5th, while the diminished fifth places it upon the 2d degree. It is therefore a real *chromatic chord*, not to be found in any diatonic scale. Thus: the chord of the seventh, or seventh and ninth, of the 7th degree in C major, occurs in A minor upon the 2d degree, and has in both cases a diminished fifth. If we alter the minor into a *major* third, the chord will seemingly belong to the scale of E minor, or E major; but in reality it must be treated as standing upon the 2d degree in A minor, and, accordingly, be succeeded by the dominant harmony, resolving into the tonic triad of that scale.

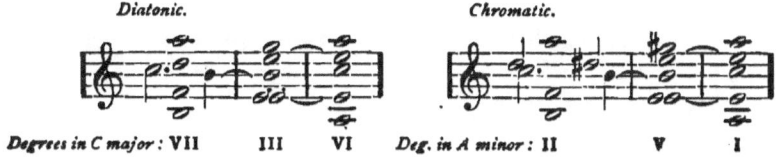

Diatonic. *Chromatic.*

Degrees in C major : **VII** **III** **VI** *Deg. in A minor* : **II** **V** **I**

This last example contains an interval hitherto not explained, resulting from the simultaneous sound of the major third and diminished fifth. **If** the major third occurs in the higher voice, an *augmented sixth* arises; but if the diminished fifth occurs in the higher voice, we have a *diminished third*.

The treatment will be similar in the following analogous cases:

1st.—The chord of the seventh, or seventh and ninth, of the 3d degree in C major, may be chromatically altered into that of the 2d degree in **D** minor, by lowering its perfect into a diminished fifth, and by raising its minor to a major third; to be followed by the dominant and tonic triads of the same scale.

2d.—The same course may be pursued with the chord of the seventh and ninth of the 6th degree in C major, with the additional alteration of the major into the minor ninth; this chord may then be treated as standing upon the 2d degree of G minor.

3d.—The same method may be observed with the chord of the seventh and ninth of the 2d degree in C major, when it may be treated as standing upon the 2d degree in C minor.

4th.—We may proceed in like manner with the chord of the seventh and ninth of the 5th degree in C major, when it may be treated as standing upon the 2d degree in F minor.

The following examples illustrate the relationship of all these chromatic progressions to the scale of C major:

II. *Diatonic.*

Chromatic.

The harshness of these chromatic chords of the seventh and ninth is easily avoided by the omission of the fundamental tone. This omission causes the chromatic chords of the seventh and ninth to sound (in the tempered system) like dominant chords of the seventh, the only difference being, that they are differently resolved.

SECTION XVII.

The resolution of these chromatic chords of the seventh and ninth, without fundamental, into the harmony of the major triad of the next fundamental, depends (if the ninth resolves simultaneously with the entrance of the next fundamental) upon the following position of the component tones, viz: the seventh of the (tacit) fundamental must be in the lowest voice ; the ninth next above ; above this, the diminished fifth, and the major third in the highest voice, as in the following example :

Diatonic.

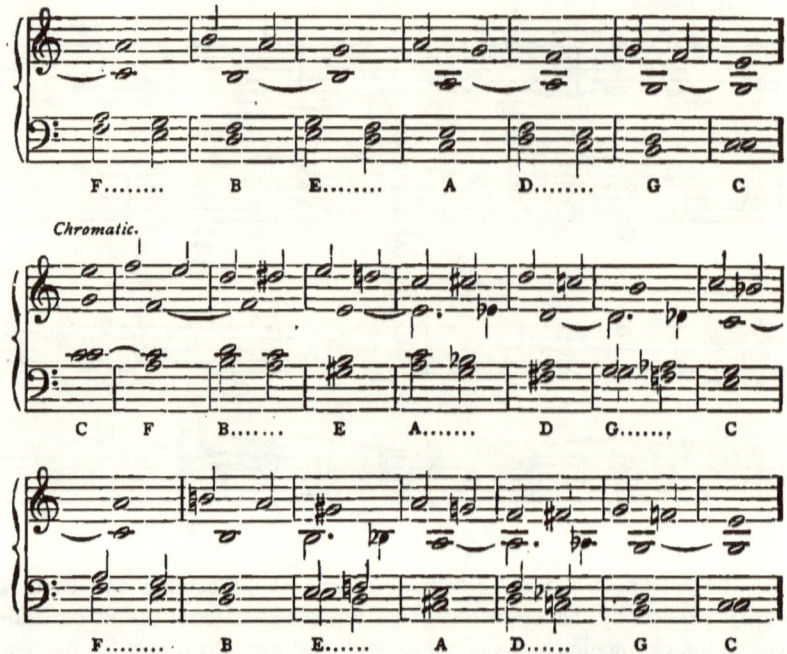

The delay of the resolution of the ninth into the fifth of the following fundamental, is best accompanied by the delay of the resolution of the seventh into the third; both remaining suspended as thirteenth and eleventh of the next fundamental, until they resolve according to rule. Here the position is immaterial, as the fundamentals of the chords of the seventh and ninth are generally inaudible.

D............   G...............   C................   F   B

E.........   A..............   D...............   G............   C

SECTION XVIII.

The perfect fifth of a chromatic chord of the seventh and ninth may be lowered to a diminished fifth, before the major third is changed into a minor third.   In the following example, the chromatic alterations, as at (b), will be found amply justified by the diatonic progressions, as at (a).

Diatonic. (a)

C   F   B   E   A   D

G   C   A   D......   G   C

Chromatic. (b)

C   F   B.......   E...........   A..........   D.........

G   C........ A   D.........   G   C

SECTION XIX.

Another license in chromatic progression is, that instead of a triad, capable of becoming a dominant, a chord of the seventh, or of the seventh and ninth, may enter free, provided it is followed by its relative tonic.

1st.—The triad of the 1st degree of C major cannot be succeeded *diatonically* by a chord of the seventh, or of the seventh and ninth, of the 3d degree, but *chromatically*, if C, E and A are treated as 3d, 5th and 1st degrees in A minor.

2d.—The triad of the 4th degree of C major cannot be succeeded *diatonically* by a chord of the seventh, or of the seventh and ninth, of the 6th degree, but *chromatically*, if F, A and D are treated as 3d, 5th and 1st degrees in D minor.

3d.—The triad of the 6th degree of C major cannot be succeeded *diatonically* by a chord of the seventh, or of the seventh and ninth, of the 1st degree, but *chromatically*, if A, C and F are treated as 3d, 5th and 1st degrees in F major.

4th.—The triad of the 7th degree cannot, as we have seen, be altered into a dominant triad. The triad of the 5th degree, however, may be succeeded by the major triad of the 7th degree, provided that this latter is followed by the triad of the 3d degree. Such a case would be, *e. g.*, in C major, if G, B, and E were treated as 3d, 5th and 1st degrees in E minor. But this progression must be regarded only as a license, being foreign to the nature of the scale of C major.

5th.—In the following chromatic progression, at *N.B.*, the diminished triad of the 7th degree seems to be followed by the harmony of the chord of the seventh of the 5th degree of G major; upon examination of the fundamentals it will be found, however, that the seeming fundamental of the triad of the 7th degree is but a passing tone arising from the fundamental D.

The following example shows the relationship of all these chromatic progressions to the scale of C major.

SECTION XX.

The chromatic progressions remaining, being of a very complicated nature, can be explained only by showing how one gives rise to another. In the following diatonic progression, containing the most important fundamentals of the scale of C major in this order: C, F, D, G, C,—C and F may be treated as dominant and tonic of F minor—F, D, and G, as 4th, 2d and 5th degrees of C minor, D as dominant of G minor, resolving into G major, to be treated as dominant of C major, ultimately to resolve into the tonic triad of that scale.

Another variation arises, if the dominant ninth in F minor remains as thirteenth of F, and if the minor triad of F stands for the chord of the seventh of the 2d degree of C minor, to be succeeded by the dominant chord of the seventh and ninth of G minor; and if the seventh of this chord remains suspended as eleventh of G, resolving into the tonic triad of G major, to close with that of C major.

Still another variation arises, if the thirteenth of F resolves, simultaneously with the passage of the other voices, into the harmony of D, which may be treated at once as dominant of G minor, thereby shortening the progression by one measure.

Now, the thirteenth of F may remain suspended, even until the entrance of the harmony of D (dominant of G minor) is effected, thereby introducing tones belonging to two different scales not related.

This last example contains an interval which has not yet been mentioned, viz : the *diminished sixth*, occurring here between *f♯* and *d♭* (*f* and *d♭* forming already a *minor* sixth). The inversion (*d♮* and *f♯*) gives an *augmented third*, since *d♭* and *f* form already a major third.

The last progression may be varied again, if, with the thirteenth of F, the octave remains suspended after the entrance of the major third of D, giving the simultaneous sound of *f♯* and *f* (a *diminished octave*, whose inversion forms an *augmented prime*).

SECTION XXI.

The nature of chromatic progression enables every degree but the seventh to stand as a tonic, provided the fundamentals succeed each other in such order that each is independent of the other. The following succession of fundamentals, with their triads, will be found of most practical use, viz : C, G, E, A, F, D, G, C.

This succession may be justified thus :

1st.—C, having stood in the outset as tonic, may be treated as sub-dominant of G major, to be followed by the tonic of that scale.

2d.—G, having stood as tonic, may be treated as 3d degree of E minor, to be followed by the tonic of that scale.

3d.—F, having stood as tonic, the A following may be treated as 4th degree of the same scale, unless we treat E as 5th degree of A minor, and A as tonic of that scale.

4th.—A, having stood as tonic, may be treated as 3d degree of F major, to be followed by the tonic of that scale.

5th.—F, having stood as tonic, may be treated as 3d degree of D minor, to be followed by the tonic of that scale.

6th.—D, having stood as tonic, may be treated as 2d degree of C major, to be followed by G, as dominant of that scale.

7th.—G, having stood as dominant of C, may now be treated as tonic of G major.

8th.—G, having stood as tonic, may now be treated as dominant of C major, to be followed by the tonic of that scale.

The recognition of a triad as tonic triad, depends upon its connection with its dominant or sub-dominant harmony, or with both.

By way of illustration of the foregoing, we give the following succession of diatonic triads in C major, forming, as it were, a theme for chromatic variations.

THEME.

First variation : Each triad may become a tonic, during the continuance of the same measure, if followed by its dominant, which being a secondary harmony, the progression cannot be considered a real fundamental one in C major.

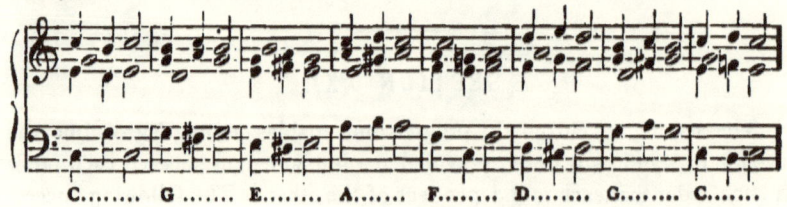

Second variation : Each triad may become a tonic, during the continu-ance of the same measure, if followed by its sub-dominant, the latter, as secondary harmony, arising also outside of the real fundamental progression.

Third variation : Each tonic (primary or secondary) may be succeeded by the (secondary) harmonies of its 4th, 2d and 5th degrees, which latter three occur again outside of the real fundamental progression :

Not to give all the other possible variations, we may state, once for all, that the first bass-note of each measure may be treated as primary fundamen-tal, to be succeeded by all its secondary fundamentals.

Each triad of the diatonic theme may also be treated as standing upon the 5th degree of a relative minor scale, and, accordingly, be succeeded by the tonic of such scale.

SECTION XXII.

The *organ-point* (*tasto solo*) is a preparation of the close of a more extended composition, and consists in the sounding of the dominant or tonic of the scale by the lowest voice, while the upper voices form a regular harmonic progression.

The organ-point must conclude with the same harmony with which it commenced, viz: with that of the dominant, if it commenced with the dominant, or, with that of the tonic, if it commenced with the tonic. This may at once be tried with the theme given in the last Section, in which the tone C, as being the leading fundamental, may continue throughout the eight measures, while the other voices make the regular progressions. It should be observed, that, if the same progressions are to be employed as an organ-point upon the *dominant,* at least *one measure* should precede, *in which that harmony is clearly heard.* However, in all the variations we have suggested, the leading fundamentals (indicated by capitals) may always remain audible throughout the measure.

————

SECTION XXIII.

Of all the scales related to C major, E minor is, so to speak, the least congenial to it, and the occurrence of its characteristic harmonies in conjunction with those of C major, has in Section XXI been to some extent justified, on the ground that the major harmony of B, as dominant of E minor, occurs simply as secondary harmony.

The student should now attempt to apply the chromatic steps explained' in this part, to the several exercises suggested in Part First.

These exercises should be worked out in the different major scales : care being taken to apply the chromatic progressions as well to the inverted as. to the primary chords.

But in order to show how these secondary scales may be again transformed into chromatic scales, we must first treat of the chromatic progressions in A minor.

PART V.

CHROMATIC PROGRESSIONS IN THE SCALE OF A MINOR.

SECTION I.

The explanation of the chromatic progressions in C major, is partly adaptable to those in A minor.

The chromatic scale of A minor *ascends* as follows : *a, b♭, b♮, c, c♯, d, d♯, e, f, f♯, g, g♯* and *a* ; hence it is identical with the chromatic scale ascending of C major, and is made up of the tones of the minor scales of A, E and D.

The *descending* chromatic scale of A minor is composed most usually of the same tones as the ascending scale. The case may occur, however, when it should descend as follows : *a, a♭, g, f♯, f♮, e, e♭, d, d♭, c, b, b♭* and *a*, in so far as it enters into relation with the scales of C, F and G major, and of C, F and G minor. And since the succession of the fundamentals : A, D, G, C, F, B, E, A (in the tempered system) remains the same, whether occurring in A minor, or in C major, it is natural, that the chromatic progression descending should remain the same in both A minor and C major, and become distinct only at the close.

SECTION II.

The principal difference between the chromatic progressions of C major and those of A minor, lies in the tones *f♯* and *g♯*, which are diatonic tones in A minor, and may be used (under restrictions) as fundamentals ; thereby affording a closer relationship to E minor and E major, and to D and A major, than could have been attained as long as C major was the leading scale. For, in the same way as the fundamental, F♯ (raised 6th degree in A minor), may be treated as the 2d degree in E minor, just so may (in the tempered system) the fundamental, B (2d degree in A minor), be treated as the 5th degree in E minor, or E major. It follows from this, that E, which in A minor is fundamental to a minor, as well as to a major triad, may be treated as 1st degree in E minor, or E major.

Since the 6th and 7th degrees are variable in the diatonic minor scale, it follows, that these two degrees may be altered, even in the chromatic progression, if they occur as fundamentals,—hence another difference between the chromatic progressions of the minor and those of the major scale. The tones, $f\sharp$ and $g\sharp$, from A minor, establish also a relationship to A major and D major. The chromatic scale of A minor, therefore, embraces the scales of A, E, and D minor; C, G and F major, A, D and E major, and C, G and F minor.

SECTION III.

In order to avoid repetitions of the explanations given in the treatise on the chromatic progressions in C major (including the allusions bearing upon the tempered system), and yet to elucidate clearly the mode of effecting chromatic progressions in the scale of A minor, we append the following:

1st.—The triad of the 1st degree of A minor (*A–c–e*) may be used unaltered for the scales of C major, F major, G major, and E minor; but its minor third must be raised to a major third, if it is to be treated as occurring in A major, or as dominant triad of D minor, or D major. Its alteration into the characteristic triad of the 2d degree of G minor is effected by the lowering of its perfect, to a diminished, fifth.

2d.—The *diminished* triad of the 2d degree of A minor (*B–d–f*) needs no alteration, to be adaptable to the scales of C major, C minor, and D minor.

3d.—The *minor* triad of the 2d degree of A minor (*B–d–f♯*) may be used unaltered for the scales of G, D, and A major; but its alteration into the dominant triad of E minor, or E major, is effected by the change of its minor, into a major, third.

4th.—The *major triad* of the 3d degree of A minor (*C–e–g*) may be employed without alteration for the scales of C, G, and F major, and those of E, D, and F minor; its alteration into the characteristic triad of the 4th degree of G minor, and its adaptation for C minor, is effected by the lowering of its major, to a minor, third.

5th.—The *augmented triad* of the 3d degree of A minor (*C–e–g♯*) is a special characteristic of this scale.

6th.—The *minor triad* of the 4th degree of A minor (*D–f–a*) may be employed unaltered for the scales of C major, F major, and D minor; its alteration into the characteristic triad of the 2d degree of C minor is effected by the change of its perfect, into a diminished, fifth.

7th.—The *major triad* of the 4th degree of A minor (*D–f♯–a*) needs no alteration to be adaptable for the scales of A, D, and G major, and those of G and E minor; but it may be altered (by license) into that of the 3d degree of B minor, by changing its perfect, into an augmented, fifth.

8th.—The *minor triad* of the 5th degree of A minor (*E–g–b*) may be used unaltered for the scales of C major, G major, D major, and E minor; but its alteration for the scale of F major or F minor, or into the characteristic triad of the 2d degree of D minor, must be effected by the change of its perfect, into a diminished, fifth.

9th.—The *major triad* of the 5th degree of A minor (*E–g♯–b*) may be employed unaltered for the scales of A and E major.

10th.—The triad of the *natural* 6th degree of A minor (*F–a–c*) may be used unaltered for the scales of C and F major; its change into the characteristic triad of the 3d degree of D minor is effected by the alteration of its perfect, into an augmented, fifth; and its recognizable change for the scales of C and F minor is effected by the alteration of its major, into a minor, third.

11th.—The triad of the *raised* 6th degree of A minor (*F♯–a–c*) may be employed unaltered for the scales of G major, G minor and E minor. It cannot be adapted for the scales of E major, D major and A major, because its diminished fifth cannot be changed into a perfect fifth.

12th.—The triad of the *natural* 7th degree of A minor (*G–b–d*) may be used unaltered for the scales of C major, G major, D major and C minor. Its adaptation for the scales of F major and D minor must be effected by the change of its major, into a minor, third, while its adaptation for the scale of F minor requires the additional change of its perfect, into a diminished, fifth. Its adaptation for the scale of E minor may be effected by the change of its perfect, into an augmented, fifth; but this is a license, since the fifth of the 7th degree should resolve one degree downward.

13th.—The triad of the *raised* 7th degree of A minor (*G♯–b–d*) needs no alteration for the scale of A major.

The chromatic alteration of the chords of the seventh, and of the seventh and ninth, of A minor, into chords of the seventh, and of the seventh and ninth, of relative scales, may be easily made, if the directions given for the chromatic alteration of the triads are adhered to. It should not be forgotten, however, that no raised degree can ever become a seventh or a ninth.

SECTION IV.

The following table will show, that the diatonic tones of the scale of A minor are fully adequate to indicate the most important fundamentals of its relative scales.

The tones *D, B, E, A*, are, in A minor, the degrees. . . . . . 4, 2, 5, 1.
in A major, the same . . . . 4, 2, 5, 1.

The tones *A, F♯, B, E*, are, in A minor, the degrees. . . . . 1, ♭, 2, 5.
in E minor, and E major, the degrees 4, 2, 5, 1.

The tones *G, E, A, D,* are, in A minor, the degrees . . . . . 7, 5, 1, 4.
in D minor, and D major, the degrees 4, 2, 5, 1.

The tones *F, D, G, C*, are, in A minor, the degrees . . . . . 6, 4, 7, 3.
in C major, and C minor, the degrees 4, 2, 5, 1.

The tones *C, A, D, G*, are, in A minor, the degrees . . . . . 3, 1, 4, 7.
in G major, and G minor, the degrees 4, 2, 5, 1.

The tones *D, G, C, F,* are, in A minor, the degrees . . . . . 4, 7, 3, 6.
in F major, the degrees . . . . . 6, 2, 5, 1.

The tones *G, C, F,* are, in A minor, the degrees . . . . . 7, 3, 6.
in F minor, the degrees . . . . . 2, 5, 1.

The tonic, dominant, and subdominant are the most important fundamentals : the triad of the last of these may be represented by the chord of the seventh of the 2d degree, whence the formula (closing cadence) IV, V, I, or II, V, I, arises. It will be better, of course, if all four fundamentals are represented.

It should be mentioned here, that the several relative scales contain even a still greater number of tones in common with A minor than the above named, viz. :

The tones : *a, g, f, e, d, c, b, a,* form
in A minor, the degrees . . 8, 7, 6, 5, 4, 3, 2, 1.
and in C major . . . . 13, 12, 11, 10, 9, 8, 7, 6.
or : 6, 5, 4, 3, 2, 1, 7, 6.

The tones : *a, b, c, d, e, f♯, g,* form
in A minor, the degrees . . . . . 1, 2, 3, 4, 5, ♭, 7.
and in G major . . . . 2, 3, 4, 5, 6, 7, 8.

The tones : *c, d, e, f, g, a,* form
in A minor, the degrees . . . . 3, 4, 5, 6, 7, 8.
and in F major . . . . 5, 6, 7, 8, 9, 10.

The tones : *e, f♯, g, a, b, c,* form
      in A minor, the degrees . . . .   5, 6, 7, 8, 9, 10.
      and in E minor . . . .   1, 2, 3, 4, 5, 6.

The tones : *d, e, f, g, a,* form
      in A minor, the degrees . . . .   4, 5, 6, 7, 8.
      and in D minor . . . .   1, 2, 3, 4, 5.

The tones : *d, e, f♯, g♯, a, b,* form
      in A minor, the degrees . . . .   4, 5, 6, 7, 8, 9.
      and in A major, the same . . . . . .   4, 5, 6, 7, 8, 9.

The tones : *d, e, f♯, g, a, b,* form
      in A minor, the degrees . . . . . .   4, 5, 6, 7, 8, 9.
      and in D major . . . . ·. . .   1, 2, 3, 4, 5, 6.

The tones : *e, f♯, g♯, a, b,* form
      in A minor, the degrees . . . .   5, 6, 7, 8, 9.
      and in E major . . . .   1, 2, 3, 4, 5.

The tones : *f, g, a, b, c, d,* form
      in A minor, the degrees . . . . . .   6, 7, 8, 9, 10, 11.
      and in C minor . . . .   4, 5, 6, 7, 8, 9.

The tones : *c, d, e, f♯, g, a,* form
      in A minor, the degrees . . . . . .   3, 4, 5, 6, 7, 8.
      and in G minor . . . .   4, 5, 6, 7, 8, 9.

The tones : *c, d, e, f, g,* form
      in A minor, the degrees . . . .   3, 4, 5, 6, 7.
      and in F minor . . . .   5, 6, 7, 8, 9.

The fact that, in giving the above table, we aimed only to show that each scale related to A minor possesses several successive tones in common with it, will explain the circumstance that in the table the degrees of that scale do not follow in their proper order—a seeming anomaly, which, however, will disappear, if the progressions taken from the diatonic scale of A minor are altered chromatically.

SECTION V.

Diatonic progressions which admit no insertion of chromatic tones :

1st.—From the tonic triad to the dominant triad, and back:

2d.—From the tonic triad to the triad of the natural 6th degree, **and** back :

3d.—From the minor triad of the 5th, to the major triad of the 3d **degree,** and back :

4th.—From the major triad of the 5th, to the augmented triad of **the 3d** degree ; the latter to be followed by the triad of the 1st, or of the **natural** 6th degree :

5th.—From the major triad of the 3d, to the chord of the seventh of **the** 1st degree (*a*).

6th.—From the triad of the natural 6th, to the minor chord of the seventh of the 4th degree (*b*) :

7th.—From the triad of the natural 7th, to the minor chord of the seventh of the 5th degree (*c*) :

8th.—From the triad of the raised 7th degree, to the dominant **chord** of the seventh (*d*) :

9th.—From the minor triad of the 4th to the chord of the seventh of the 2d degree (*e*) :

10th.—From the minor triad of the 5th, to the major chord of the seventh of the 3d degree (*f*) :

11th.—From the diminished triad of the 2d, to the chord of the seventh of the natural or raised 7th degree (*g*) :

12th.—From the tonic triad to the chord of the seventh of the natural or raised 6th degree (*h*) :

13th.--From the chord of the seventh of the 2d degree to the dominant chord of the seventh :

14th.—From the minor triad, or chord of the seventh, of the 4th, to the chord of the seventh of the raised 7th degree :

15th.—From the harmony of the chord of the seventh of the raised 7th, to that of the augmented triad, or chord of the seventh, of the 3d degree, resolving into the harmony of the natural 6th degree :

16th.—From the major triad of the 3d to that of the natural 6th degree :

17th.—From the triad of the 1st, to the major triad of the 3d degree :

18th.—From the minor triad of the 4th, to the triad of the natural 6th degree :

19th.—From the seeming step of the diminished triad of the 2d, to the minor triad of the 4th degree, when the latter stands for the chord of the seventh of the 2d degree :

20th.—From the seeming step of the minor triad of the 5th, to the triad of the natural 7th degree, when the latter stands for the minor chord of the seventh of the 5th degree :

E............

SECTION VI.

The most simple chromatic progressions in A minor are the following :

	Diatonic.	Chromatic.	Diatonic.	Chromatic.
1.—I. IV.				

Degrees in A minor: I   IV   I   IV
  "   " D minor: V   I   V   I

Diatonic.   Chromatic.

2.—II. V.

Degrees in A minor: II   V
  "   " E minor: V   —   V   —   I
  "   " E major: V   I   V   I

Diatonic.   Chromatic.

3.—VI. II.

Degrees in A minor: VI   II   Degrees in D minor: III   ♮VI

Diatonic.   Chromatic.

4.—VI. III.

Degrees in A minor: VI   III   Degrees in C minor: IV
  "   " C major: IV   I   "   " F minor: I   V
  "   " F "   I   V

Diatonic.   Chromatic.

5.—III. VI.

Degrees in A minor: III   VI   Degrees in F major :   V   I
  "   " C major: I   IV

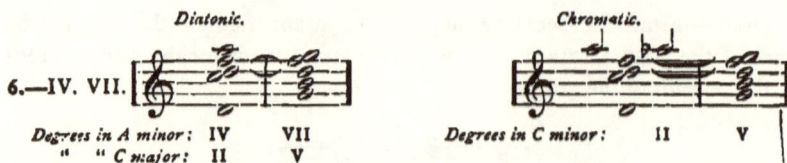

6.—IV. VII.

Diatonic.

Chromatic.

| Degrees in A minor: | IV | VII |
| " " C major: | II | V |

| Degrees in C minor: | II | V |

These chromatic progressions will present no difficulty to those who have attentively studied the diatonic progressions in the minor scale, and the chromatic steps in the major scale, as we have explained them.

SECTION VII.

The following are complex progressions :

1st.—From the chord of the seventh of the 5th degree, with minor third, to the chord of the seventh of the 1st, and thence to the minor triad of the 4th degree. The 1st and 2d fundamentals may here be treated as 2d and 5th degrees of a relative minor scale, if the fifth of the 1st chord is lowered, and the third of the 2d chord is raised, when the 3d fundamental at once becomes a tonic.

Diatonic.

Chromatic.

| Degrees in A minor: | V | I | IV |
| " " C major: | III | VI | II |

| Degrees in D minor: | II | V | I |

This example may be made more chromatic, if the second and third fundamentals are treated as dominant and tonic of D major. In this way, the triad of D major may be followed by that of D minor.

| Degrees in D minor: | | II | V | | I |
| " " D major: | II | | V | I | |

2d.—From the chord of the seventh of the raised 6th, to the minor triad of the 2d, and thence to the major triad of the 5th degree.

Diatonic.

Chromatic.

| Degrees in A minor: | ♯VI | II | V |

| Degrees in E minor: | II | V | |
| " " E major: | | V | I |

The last example becomes more chromatic, if the second fundamental is followed, first by the minor, and then by the major triad of the last fundamental, thus rendering the chromatic progression more complicated, *e. g.*:

Degrees in E minor: II   V   I
"   " E major: V   I

3d.—From the chord of the seventh of the natural 7th, to that of the 3d, and thence to the triad of the natural 6th degree.

Degrees in A minor: VII   III   VI   Degrees in F major: II   V   I
"   " C major: V   I   IV   "   " D minor: IV   VII   III

Degrees in F minor: II   V
"   " F major: II   V   I

4th.—From the chord of the seventh of the 1st, to that of the 4th, thence to that of the natural 7th, and thence to the triad of the 3d degree.

Degrees in A minor: I   IV   VII   III
"   " C major: VI   II   V   I

Degrees in G major: II   V
"   " C   "   VI   II   V   I

Degrees in G major: II   V
"   " G minor: II   V
"   " C minor: II   V
"   " C major: VI   II   V   I

5th.—From the triad of the 1st, to the minor triad of the 5th, thence to the chord of the seventh of the 1st, and thence to the minor triad of the 4th degree.

This example becomes more chromatic, if the last fundamental exhibits first a major, and then a minor triad.

6th.—From the chord of the seventh of the raised 6th, to the minor triad of the 2d degree, thence to the dominant chord of the seventh, and thence to the tonic triad.

7th.—From the dominant chord of the seventh, to the tonic triad, and thence to the dominant triad.

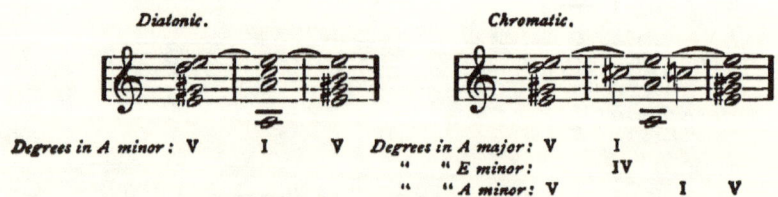

8th.—From the tonic triad to the minor triad of the 5th, thence to the chord of the seventh of the 3d, and thence to the triad of the natural 6th degree.

Diatonic.

Chromatic.

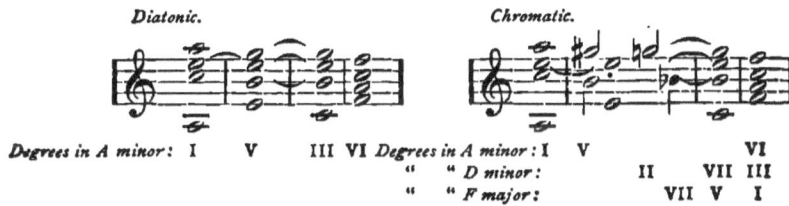

Degrees in A minor: I V III VI *Degrees in A minor:* I V VI
" " *D minor:* II VII III
" " *F major:* VII V I

SECTION VIII.

The following connected examples will show, that the chromatic progressions explained in Sections VI and VII, are related to the scale of A minor.

I. *Diatonic.*

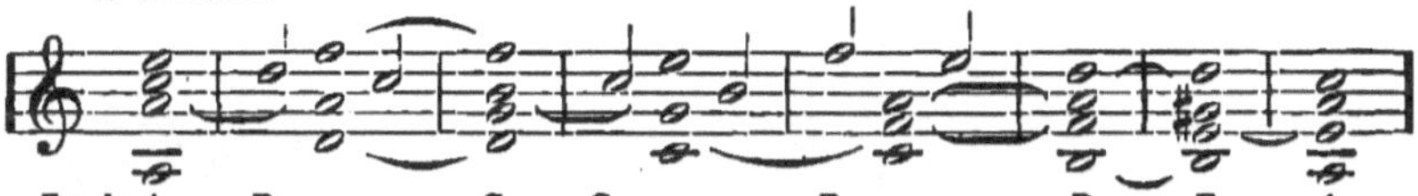

Fund. A D......... G C.......... F......... B E A

Chromatic, with the same fundamental progression.

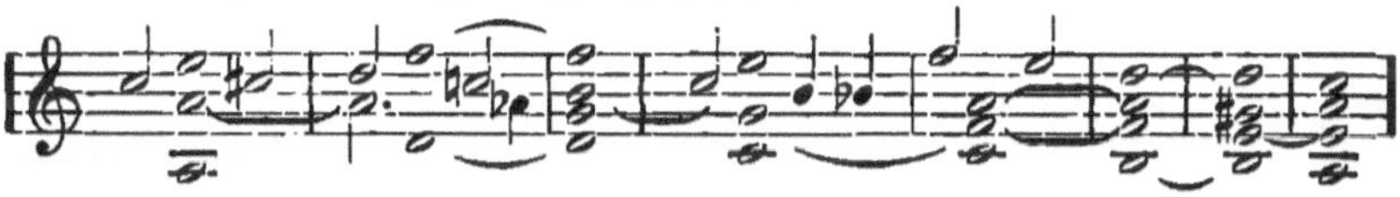

II. *Diatonic.*

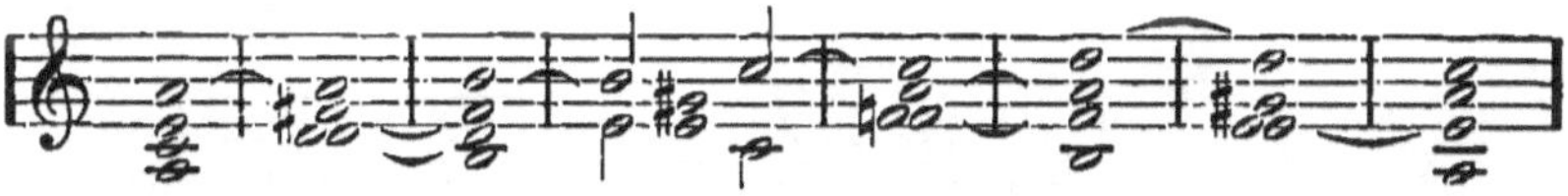

Chromatic.

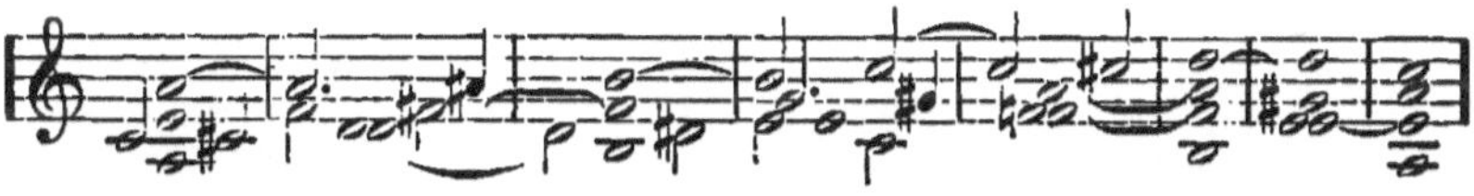

III. *Diatonic.*

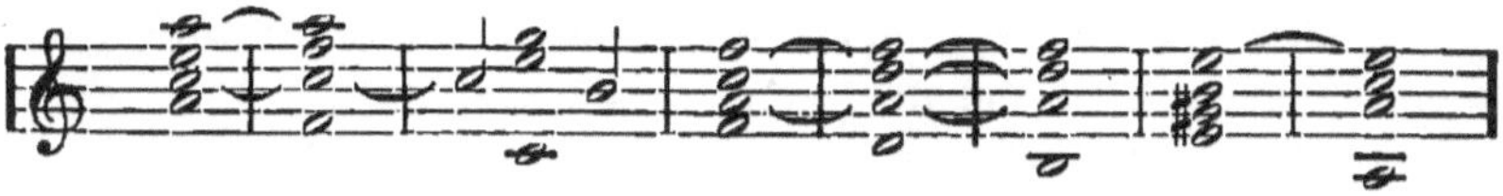

Chromatic.

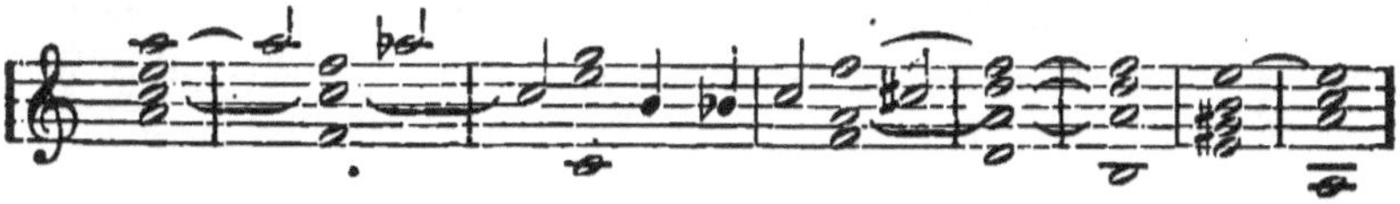

IV. *Diatonic.*

Chromatic.

V. *Diatonic.*

Chromatic.

VI. *Diatonic.*

Chromatic.

SECTION IX.

We must now show what progresssions admit the use of the natural, instead of the raised, 6th and 7th degrees in the fundamental.

1st.—From the harmony of the augmented triad of the 3d, to the chord of the seventh of the raised 6th degree; thence to the harmony of the chord of the seventh of the 4th degree, with major third; thence to the triad of the raised 7th degree; thence to the harmony of the chord of the dominant seventh, to terminate with the tonic triad. Here the natural, instead of the raised 6th degree, may stand as second fundamental; but the third fundamental occurs with a major third. The natural, instead of the raised 7th degree, will occur as fourth fundamental, while the fifth fundamental appears with a major third, and resolves naturally into the harmony of the last fundamental. The augmented harmony of the 3d degree is best preceded (in diatonic, as well as in chromatic harmony), by the dominant harmony, which again is preceded by the tonic triad.

2d. —If the tonic triad is immediately followed by the chord of the seventh of the raised 6th degree, etc., as in the last example, the same chromatic changes may be made.

3d.—From the tonic triad to the chord of the seventh of the 4th degree, with a major third; thence to the harmony of the triad of the raised 7th degree, thence to the dominant harmony, resolving into that of the tonic triad.

We are free to choose the raised, instead of the natural 6th degree, as fundamental, if it is preceded by the major harmony of the 3d, and followed by the chord of the seventh of the 2d degree, etc.   The harmonies of the 3d, raised 6th, and 2d degrees, may then be treated as those of the natural 6th, 2d, and 5th degrees in E minor.   The return to A minor requires only the lowering of the major third of the 2d degree into a minor third, and of the perfect fifth into a diminished fifth, whereby the harmony of the 5th degree in E minor is again altered into that of the 2d degree in A minor, to be followed by its dominant and tonic.

SECTION X.

We have already, in treating of the chromatic progressions in the **major** scale, sufficiently explained the privileges of the dominant chord of the **seventh**, and of the seventh and ninth, in regard both to the leading and **the** related secondary scales : hence, the following examples in minor **will** require no additional explanation.

I. Diatonic, with returning motions :

Chromatic, with dominant chords of the seventh of the related secondary scales :

Chromatic, with chords of the seventh and ninth, etc. :

II. Diatonic, with the resolution of the ninth of the first, into the **fifth** of the second fundamental :

Chromatic, with the same fundamentals:

III. Diatonic, in which the second and fourth fundamentals admit **only** a triad:

Chromatic, in which the second and fourth fundamentals admit the free entrance of a dominant chord of the seventh:

Chromatic, in which the same fundamentals admit the free entrance of a chord of the seventh and ninth; this being best effected by omitting the fundamental tone.

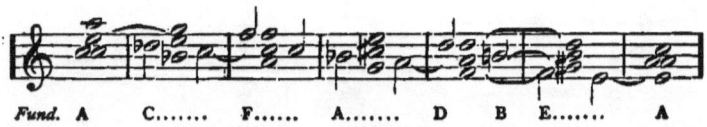

Fund. **A   C.......   F......   A.......   D   B   E.......   A**

SECTION XI.

The formation of chromatic chords of the seventh, and of the seventh and ninth, seemingly standing upon the 5th degree, because of their major third, but in reality standing upon the 2d degree of a relative minor scale, because of their diminished fifth (Section XVI, Part IV), will now be ex-emplified in the scale of A minor.

I. From the chord of the seventh of the 2d degree, to the dominant triad, closing with the tonic triad.

When the chord of the seventh of the natural 6th degree precedes, the chord of the seventh and ninth of the 2d degree may follow, and the seventh of the 6th degree may resolve into the major, instead of the minor third of the 2d degree. This major third of the 2d degree must be lowered to a minor third, if the dominant chord of the seventh is to follow, in order that the seventh may be prepared.

In this last example, the ninth of the 2d degree resolves during the continuance of the same fundamental. If it is to resolve into the fifth of the following fundamental, it must be placed in the most favorable position, as in the following example:

The same favorable position is necessary, if the chord of the seventh and ninth of the 2d degree is to be followed by the dominant triad.

Should the position of the voices be unfavorable for the progression alluded to, the only way to avoid faulty progressions would be to suspend the seventh and ninth of the 2d degree, as eleventh and thirteenth of the next fundamental.

II. From the dominant chord of the seventh, to the tonic triad, and thence to the subdominant triad:

If the first chord is a chord of the seventh and ninth, it may become a chromatic chord of the 2d degree in D minor, by the alteration of its perfect into a diminished fifth:

The following examples illustrate the resolution of the ninth into the fifth of the following fundamental, in the favorable position, (*a*), and the suspension of the seventh and ninth, as eleventh and thirteenth, in the unfavorable position (*b*).

III. From the chord of the seventh of the 1st, to the minor triad of the 4th degree, thence to the chord of the seventh of the natural 7th, closing with the major triad of the 3d degree:

If the first chord is a chord of the seventh and ninth, it may become a chromatic chord of the 2d degree in G minor, by the alteration of its major into a minor ninth, its minor into a major third, and of its perfect into a diminished fifth.

The resolution of the ninth into the fifth of the following fundamental, in the favorable position, and the suspension of the seventh and ninth as eleventh and thirteenth, in the unfavorable position, require no farther illustration.

IV. From the minor chord of the seventh of the 4th degree, to the triad of the natural 7th degree (by way of returning motion), thence to the chord of the seventh of the 3d, closing with the triad of the natural 6th degree:

Degrees in A minor: IV   VII   III   VI
"   " C major: II   V   I   IV

Degrees in F major: VI   II   V   I
"   " G minor: V   I
"   " C minor: II   V
"   " F minor: II   V

If the first chord is a chord of the seventh and ninth, it may become a chromatic chord of the 2d degree in C minor, by the alteration of its major into a minor ninth, of its minor into a major third, and of its perfect into a diminished fifth.

V. From the chord of the seventh of the natural 7th degree, to the major triad of the 3d, thence to the triad of the natural 6th degree:

| *Degrees in A minor:* | VII | III | VI | *Degrees in F major:* | V | | |
| " " C major: | V | I | IV | " " F minor: II | V | I |

If the first chord is a chord of the seventh and ninth, it may become a chromatic chord of the 2d degree in F minor, by the alteration of the major into a minor ninth, and of the perfect into a diminished fifth.

SECTION XII.

The following connected examples will show that all the chromatic progressions explained in the last Section are related to the scale of A minor.

1st.—The resolution of the ninth into the fifth of the succeeding fundamental.

2d.—The suspension of the seventh and ninth, as eleventh and thirteenth of the succeeding fundamental:

SECTION XIII.

The theme introducing the fundamentals in such order, that their triads may be treated as tonic triads, is not the same in the minor as in the major scale, since the triad of the 2d degree in the former cannot become a tonic. On the other hand, the triad of the natural 7th degree (in the tempered system) may become a tonic.

The following two orders of fundamentals may be made use of:

        First order :   A, E, C, F, D, B, E, A.
        Second order :   A, D, G, C, F, B, E, A.

Justification of the *first order :*

1st.—The fundamental, A, having stood as tonic, may also be treated as sub-dominant of E minor, to be followed by the tonic of that scale.

2d.—E, having stood as tonic, may also be treated as 3d degree of C major, to be followed by the tonic of that scale.

3d.—C, having stood as tonic, may also be treated as dominant of F major, to be followed by the tonic of that scale.

4th.—F, having stood as tonic, may also be treated as 3d degree of D minor, to be followed by the tonic of that scale.

5th.—D, having stood as tonic, may also be treated as sub-dominant of A minor, to be followed by the 2d degree of that scale (B).

6th.—Since B cannot become a tonic, on account of its diminished fifth, it must be followed at once by E, as dominant of A minor, involving, accordingly, a major third.

7th.—The major triad of E, having stood as dominant of A minor, may also be treated as tonic of E major.

8th.—E, having stood as tonic, may now be treated as dominant of A minor, to be followed by A, as leading tonic.

The following succession of diatonic triads in A minor, will serve as an illustration of the above order.

THEME.

First variation, introducing each triad of the theme as tonic for one measure, during which it is followed by its own dominant harmony, which latter, as secondary harmony, forms no part of the fundamental progression.

Second variation, in which each triad is followed by its sub-dominant harmony, this being also foreign to the regular fundamental progression.

Third variation, in which, during one measure, every tonic is followed by the harmonies of its sub-dominant, 2d degree, and dominant, which also, as secondary, form no part of the regular fundamental progression.

Fourth variation, in which each measure contains a leading fundamental, followed by all its secondary fundamentals.

The capitals everywhere indicate the leading fundamentals, which are sounded at the beginning and end of each measure, the intermediate chords being regarded as the harmonies of secondary fundamentals, and, as such, forming no part of the regular fundamental progression.

SECTION XIV.

Justification of the *second order* of fundamentals.

1st.—A, having stood as tonic, is followed by D, which may be treated either as sub-dominant of A minor, or as tonic.

2d.—D, having stood as tonic, may also be treated as 2d degree of C major, and be followed by its dominant, G.

3d.—G, having stood as dominant, may also be treated, first, as tonic of G major, afterwards, as dominant of C major, to be followed by the tonic of that scale.

4th.—C, having stood as tonic, may be treated as dominant of F major.

5th.—F, having stood as tonic, may be treated as 6th degree of A minor, to be followed by the 2d degree (B).

6th.—Since B cannot become a tonic, because of its diminished fifth, it must be followed at once by E, as dominant of A minor, involving, accordingly, a major third.

7th.—E, having stood as dominant of A minor, may now be treated as tonic of E major.

8th.—E, having stood as tonic of E major, may now be treated as dominant of A minor, to be followed by A, as leading tonic.

The following succession of diatonic triads will serve as an illustration of the second order :

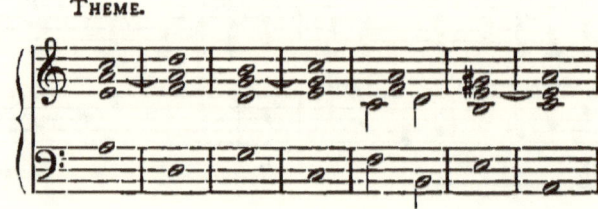

First variation, introducing each triad of the theme as tonic during **one** measure, followed by its respective sub-dominant and dominant harmonies, which, however, must be treated as secondary harmonies only:

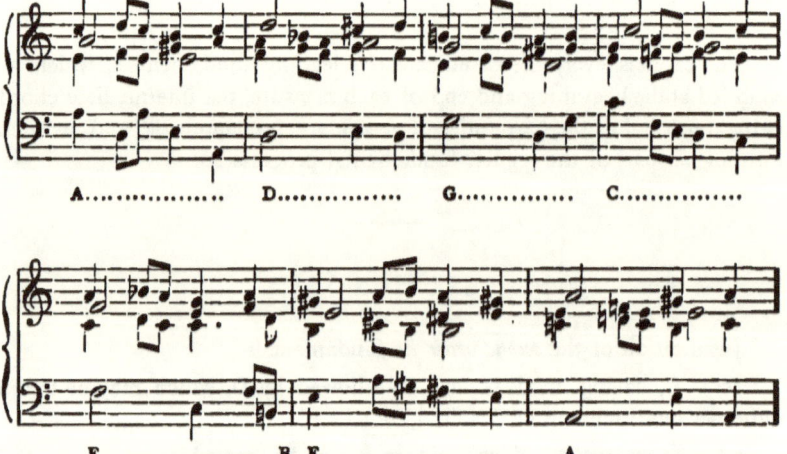

Second variation, in which the tonic of each measure is followed by the harmonies of its 6th, 2d and 5th degrees :

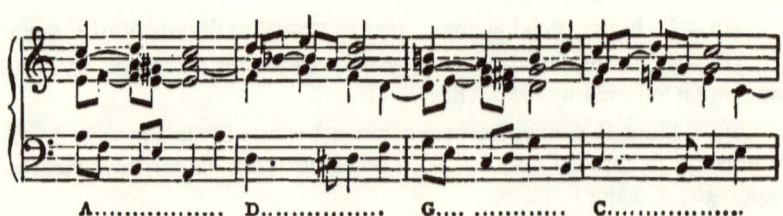

SECTION XV.

The formation of an organ-point in A minor will present no difficulty, if Section XXIII of Part IV is carefully perused, and then applied to the scale of A minor.

Here we need only to exemplify how the secondary scales may again become chromatic. For this purpose, it will suffice, to give a chromatic form to the last example but one of the preceding Section, with such alterations of the intermediate chords as are involved in the rhythmical requirements of the measure.

PART VI.

OF ENHARMONIC CHANGES.

SECTION I.

WE have shown, when speaking of the *strict* system of tuning, that a scale tuned according to this system differs materially from the same scale tuned according to the modern *equal temperament*, as it is called. Hence it is only in the latter system that two different scales—*e. g.*, C♯ and D♭—can sound exactly alike, and differ only in their notation. Since, however, the equal temperament is now generally adopted, we may, from motives of convenience,* especially in compositions for keyed-instruments, substitute one scale for another having the same sound, but a different notation,—and in this consists what is called the *enharmonic change.* The most practical enharmonic changes are the following, viz: *c♭*, for *b*; *c♯*, for *d♭*; *d♯*, for *e♭*; *f♯*, for *g♭*; *g♯*, for *a♭*; *a♯*, for *b♭*,—and *vice versa*.

For the application of enharmonic changes, it will be found convenient to arrange the different scales in musical circles, like the following:

1st.—Beginning with the scale of C major, followed by the others as they increase in the number of sharps; the 5th degree of each scale forming the 1st of the next, viz: C major, G major, D major, A major, E major, B major, F♯ major. The next scale in this order would be C♯ major. But we exchange F♯ major for G♭ major, and continue in that order in which the scales decrease in the number of flats, viz: G♭ major, D♭ major, A♭ major, E♭ major, B♭ major, F major, and C major,—which completes the circle.

---

* Among these may be mentioned, *greater facility in reading, e. g.* in A♭, rather than in G♯ major, with a signature of *eight sharps*. Again, a correctly applied enharmonic change will often clearly foreshadow a harmony whose sudden appearance, without it, could hardly be comprehended, as far as its notation is concerned.

We may also begin with A minor, proceeding as before, viz.: E minor, B minor, F♯ minor, C♯ minor, G♯ minor, D♯ minor. We then exchange D♯ minor for E♭ minor, and continue in the same order, as follows: B♭ minor, F minor, C minor, G minor, D minor and A minor, which concludes the circle.

2d.—We may begin again with C major, introducing the scales as they increase in flats, the 1st degree of each scale forming the fifth of the next, viz.: C major, F major, B♭ major, E♭ major, A♭ major, D♭ major, G♭ major. We then exchange G♭ major for F♯ major, continuing in the same order, as follows: B major, E major, A major, D major, G major and C, thereby closing the circle.

We may also begin with A minor, proceeding in like manner, as follows; D minor, G minor, C minor, F minor, B♭ minor, E♭ minor. We then exchange E♭ minor for D♯ minor, and continue as before: G♯ minor, C♯ minor, F♯ minor, B minor, E minor and A minor, thereby closing the circle.

The following examples will serve for better illustration :

Modulations from C major, proceeding in the order given under I, until C major is again reached.

Degrees. I, IV II V   I, IV II V   I, IV II V   I, etc.

Modulations from A minor, proceeding in the same order, until A minor is again reached.

Degrees. I, IV II V　　I, IV II V　　I, IV II V　　I, *etc.*

Modulations from C major, proceeding in the order given under II, until C major is again reached.

Degrees. I, V I　IV II V　I, V I　IV II V　I, V I　IV II V　I, V I, *etc.*

Modulations from A minor, proceeding in the same order, until A minor is again reached.

Degrees. I, V I   IV II V   I, V I   IV II V   I, V I   IV II V

I, V I   IV II V

N.B.

The mark *N.B.* always indicates the enharmonic changes, in these, as well as in the subsequent examples.

SECTION II.

If we wish to shorten the circle, we may modulate in the following manner:

I. We begin with C major, modulate into A minor, and conclude in A major; we then modulate into F♯ minor, concluding in F♯ major. After having exchanged F♯ major for G♭ major, we modulate into E♭ minor, and conclude in E♭ major, from whence we modulate into C minor, concluding in C major.

II. We begin with C major, modulate into E minor, and conclude in E major; we then modulate into G♯ minor, concluding in G♯ major; after having exchanged G♯ major for A♭ major, we modulate into C minor, and conclude in C major.

The following examples may serve as illustrations:

By the aid of these examples, the student will be enabled to begin and end the circle with any other scale.

The following peculiar progression will be found of service for the formation of a short circle of the minor scales:

We begin with A minor, modulating by means of the dominant into G minor; thence by the same means into F minor; thence into E♭ minor. After exchanging E♭ minor for D♯ minor, we modulate by means of the dominant into C♯ minor; thence into B minor, thence into A minor, thereby closing the circle.

We have a similar circle, if we begin and end with D minor, thus introducing the other minor scales.

SECTION III.

By means of independent triads only, we may form a short circle in the following manner:

I. We begin with the major triad of C, descending by a minor third to the minor triad of A, which latter we may treat at first as the 6th degree of C major, and then as 1st degree of A minor, when it may be followed by its dominant, the major triad of E. This triad may be followed by the minor triad of C♯, which latter we treat at first as that of the 6th degree of E major, and then as that of the 1st degree of C♯ minor, to be followed by its dominant, the major triad of G♯. After substituting for the latter chord, the major triad of A♭, we may treat this latter as tonic triad of A♭ major, to be followed by the minor triad of F; this again may be treated, at first as the triad of the 6th degree of A♭ major, and then as tonic triad of F mi-

nor, to be followed by its dominant, the major triad of C, thereby concluding the circle.

II. The triad of C major may be followed by that of C minor, and the
latter be treated as the triad of the 6th degree of E♭ major, to be followed
by the major triad of A♭, as that of the 4th, and the major triad of E♭ as
that of the 1st degree, of E♭ major. After substituting for the minor triad
of E♭ that of D♯, we may treat the latter as the triad of the 6th degree of
F♯ major, to be followed by the major triad of B, as that of the 4th, and by
the major triad of F♯ as that of the 1st degree, of F♯ major, to be altered
into the minor triad of F♯. This triad may now be treated as that of the
6th degree of A major, to be followed by the major triad of D, as that of
the 4th, and then by the major triad of A, as that of the 1st degree, of A
major, to be altered into the minor triad of A. This latter we treat as the
triad of the 6th degree of C major, to be followed at first by the major triad
of F, as that of the 4th, and then by the major triad of C, as that of the 1st
degree, of C major, thereby closing the circle.

The student should now begin and end the circle with other scales, *e. g.*:
with F major, G major, B♭ major, etc.

SECTION IV.

Enharmonic modulations are effected chiefly by means of the dominant chords of the seventh and ninth of inaudible fundamentals. In this connection it will be well to recall once more the table given in Section V of Part III, viz: ∿

Major scales: C♭, G♭, D♭, A♭, E♭, B♭, F, C, G, D, A, E, B, F♯, C♯

Minor scales: a♭, e♭, b♭, f, c, g, d, a, e, b, f♯, c♯, g♯, d♯, a♯

It must be mentioned here, that at the third step to the right, from any minor scale, the major scale of the same name is found, both possessing the same dominant harmony, which differs only in the *ninth*.

Hence arise the three following analogous series of relative scales:

I. A♭ minor and A♭ major have the same dominant, and the latter has the same tones with F minor. F minor and F major have the same dominant, and the latter has the same tones with D minor. D minor and D major have the same dominant, and the latter has the same tones with B minor. B minor and B major have the same dominant, and the latter has the same tones with G♯ minor.

II. E♭ minor and E♭ major have the same dominant, and the latter has the same tones with C minor. C minor and C major have the same dominant, and the latter has the same tones with A minor. A minor and A major have the same dominant, and the latter has the same tones with F♯ minor. F♯ minor and F♯ major have the same dominant, and the latter has the same tones with D♯ minor.

III. B♭ minor and B♭ major have the same dominant, and the latter has the same tones with G minor. G minor and G major have the same dominant, and the latter has the same tones with E minor. E minor and E major have the same dominant, and the latter has the same tones with C♯ minor. C♯ minor and C♯ major have the same dominant, and the latter has the same tones with A♯ minor.

1st.—The first series is involved in the construction of the following minor scales: A♭, F, D, B, and G♯. The consideration of the dominant chords of the seventh and ninth (of inaudible fundamentals) of each of the above named scales, will show their influence upon the modulation. Thus: the dominant of A♭ minor is *E♭*, the major third of which is *g*, its perfect fifth, *b♭*, its minor seventh, *d♭*, and its minor ninth, *f♭*. Consequently, the dominant chord of A♭ minor, omitting the fundamental, is: *g–b♭––d♭–f♭*. The dominant of F minor is *C*, the major third, perfect fifth, minor seventh and minor ninth of which are: *e, g, b♭*, and *d♭* ; omitting the fundamental, we have *e–g–b♭–d♭*. The dominant of D minor is *A*, the major third, perfect fifth, minor seventh and minor ninth of which are : $c\sharp$, e, g and $b\flat$; omitting the fundamental, we have $c\sharp\text{-}e\text{-}g\text{-}b\flat$. The dominant of B minor is $F\sharp$, the major third, perfect fifth, minor seventh and minor ninth of which are : $a\sharp$, $c\sharp$, e and g ; omitting the fundamental, we have $a\sharp\text{-}c\sharp\text{-}e\text{-}g$. The dominant of $G\sharp$ minor is $D\sharp$, the major third, perfect fifth, minor seventh and minor ninth of which are : $f\times$, $a\sharp$, $c\sharp$, and e ; omitting the fundamental, we have $f\times\text{-}a\sharp\text{-}c\sharp\text{-}e$.

If we sound successively on the pianoforte these five chords, viz.: $g\text{-}b\flat\text{-}d\flat\text{-}f\flat$; $e\text{-}g\text{-}b\flat\text{-}d\flat$; $c\sharp\text{-}e\text{-}g\text{-}b\flat$; $a\sharp\text{-}c\sharp\text{-}e\text{-}g$; and $f\times\text{-}a\sharp\text{-}c\sharp\text{-}e$; the ear will discover no difference between them : they are distinguished only by a different notation.

2d.—The explication of the above series answers also for the second series, in its application to the minor scales of E$\flat$, C, A, F$\sharp$, and D$\sharp$.

3d.—The same explanation holds good for the third series, in its application to the minor scales of B$\flat$, G, E, C$\sharp$ and A$\sharp$.

SECTION V.

Those chords of the seventh which are treated as substitutes for a dominant chord of the seventh and ninth of a tacit fundamental, are termed *enharmonic chords*, on account of their polygenous nature, as shown in the last Section. They may enter free and unprepared, and are well adapted for modulations into remote scales.

Our tempered system presents to the ear only *three* enharmonic chords of the seventh, although they can be applied to different scales, and are distinguishable only by their different notation.

In order to show how to reach any scale by means of these three enharmonic chords, we begin with that of A minor. Its immediate relatives are E minor and D minor. The triad of A minor may be followed by its own dominant chord of the seventh and ninth, without fundamental, or by that of E minor or D minor, without presenting any difficulty.

The enharmonic chord of A minor being identical in sound with that of C minor, F$\sharp$ minor, D$\sharp$ minor and E$\flat$ minor, nothing prevents their being exchanged for each other.

The enharmonic chord of E minor being identical in sound with that of G minor, B$\flat$ minor, C$\sharp$ minor, and A$\sharp$ minor, these chords, again, may be interchanged.

The enharmonic chord of D minor sounds the same as that of F minor, A$\flat$ minor, B minor and G$\sharp$ minor ; and, accordingly, may be exchanged for any of these chords.

A wider range of modulation is afforded by the circumstance that the dominant harmony of a minor scale may follow after, and lead into, a major triad. Here, however, the succession of the fundamentals is more seeming than real, since only the dominant and tonic bear some relation to each other.

The following examples show the enharmonic modulations from A minor into all the other minor scales.

N.B. The fundamental tone must in every case be omitted.

The above examples may all begin with, and again resolve into, a major triad.

SECTION VI.

Another opportunity is afforded for modulating by means of these enharmonic chords, if the ninth of the tacit fundamental remains suspended after the entrance of the tonic, so that the seeming chord which arises from the suspension, is accepted as satisfactory.

From these examples are derived the following returning motions :

The student should modulate with the two other enharmonic chords, after the manner just exemplified.

SECTION VII.

The chromatic chords of the seventh and ninth consisting of a major third, diminished fifth, minor seventh and minor ninth, which, without fundamental, sound like the harmony of the dominant seventh, furnish further means for enharmonic modulation.

It has been shown in explaining the chromatic progressions, that each chromatic chord of the seventh and ninth stands upon the 2d degree of a minor scale, and may be followed by the harmony of the major triad of the 5th degree, when it occurs in the most favorable position ; otherwise, the seventh and ninth may remain suspended as eleventh and thirteenth.

In exemplifying this in A minor, we must recollect that the chromatic chord of the seventh and ninth of the 2d degree (of a tacit fundamental), contains only the tones, *f*, *a*, *c*, and *d*♯, which sound like *f*, *a*, *c*, and *e*♭, and therefore may stand as dominant of B♭ major, or B♭ minor, while its real nature requires a resolution into the dominant of A minor, to lead in the tonic of that scale.

The harmony of the two examples at (*a*) remains in A minor; that of (*b*) begins in A minor, and ends in B♭ major; that of (*c*) begins in B♭ minor, and ends in A minor.

The fundamentals must remain inaudible.

In order that this may be better understood, we observe that the tone which in the chord of the seventh seems to be the fundamental, is in reality the diminished fifth of the tacit fundamental of the chromatic chord of the seventh and ninth.

SECTION VIII.

Each dominant chord of the seventh and ninth may be altered into a chromatic chord of the seventh and ninth, by lowering its perfect into a diminished fifth, as we have already seen. Here it may be mentioned that the chord of the seventh and ninth of the 5th degree in A minor, may enter with a minor third, to resolve into a major third. The various ways in which these progressions can be used, will be understood from the following two examples, in which the fundamentals should be inaudible.

Fundamentals:	A	E......		A	D	Fundamentals: A	D	G E....	A
Deg. in A minor:	I	V......			IV	Deg. in A min.: I	IV	VII V...	I
" " D minor:			II	V	I	" " C maj.: VI	II	V	VI

If the harmony of the second measure of the 1st example is treated enharmonically, it is possible to modulate into E♭ major, or E♭ minor.

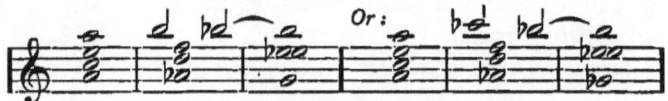

The enharmonic treatment of the 3d measure of the second example, opens the way into C minor, F♯ minor, E♭ or D♯ minor, or (in consequence of the identity of the dominant in minor and major), into C major, F♯ major, and E♭ major.

SECTION IX.

It was shown in Section XIII, Part IV, that a succession of dominant chords of the seventh and ninth may occur in a descending order, as for instance, in C major, by the following progression of fundamentals, viz : B, E, A, D, G, C, F, which may be used also in A minor. Now that we are treating of enharmonic changes, we call attention to the privilege of all enharmonic chords of the seventh (being substitutes for the dominant chords of the seventh and ninth), to enter free and unprepared, thereby admitting also an ascending succession of such chords. In this case, no other justification of the progression of fundamentals is necessary than the assertion of their polygenous nature.

SECTION X.

With regard to Section VI, it must be added, that chromatic chords of the seventh and ninth, of tacit fundamentals, may be treated on the same principle as enharmonic chords, viz.: the ninth of the tacit fundamental may remain suspended as thirteenth of the following (dominant) fundamental, and in many cases we are perfectly satisfied, even with the seeming chord which arises from the suspension.

Since we are free to close in a major scale, we may now use the privilege of altering the minor thirteenth of the 5th degree in A minor, into the major thirteenth of the 5th degree in A major, when the above harmony may be altered in the following manner:

In applying the enharmonic changes, there is not now, generally speaking, any attention paid to the proper progressions of the fundamentals (those progressions which were mentioned in Sections I–III excepted), but on the contrary, any chord whatsoever, possessing the least privilege, may be introduced arbitrarily, without special regard to the preceding harmony.

CONCLUDING REMARKS.

The diatonic harmony, major or minor, is the foundation of all good melody. It presents the picture of a family, in which every member appears in its right place, and at the right time.

The diatonic modulation introduces different related families, one after the other.

The chromatic harmony, whether the leading tonic be major or minor, renders the melody richer, and more impassioned.   It represents the subordination of several related families under one head.

The enharmonic changes, in their widest range, are the natural adversaries of a good melody, but their effect is mysterious and surprising. They represent the wide world, which dissolves the family, produces many illusions, and clothes the unsubstantial with a certain splendor, leaving it very difficult to decide, which is reality, and which is deception.